Rise of the Anointed Ones
Anointed for Such a Time

40 Days to a Deeper Walk with God
Includes Biblical Devotional Poetry

By Kenneth L. Birks

~

Published by Straight Arrow Publications
Second Edition Update 2024
www.straitarrow.net
Copyright 2022.

Cover Design by Hans Bennewitz
design / illustration / art direction
hans@modedesign.us
www.hansbennewitz.com

Unless otherwise indicated, all Scripture quotations are taken from The Holy Bible, New King James Version © 1982 by Thomas Nelson, Included

The Rise of the Anointed Ones

Given to the spirit of the times, sinful behavior normalizes.
Blinded by self-absorbed, unrighteous ones; denial demonizes.
Filled with hate and violence, the antichrist spirit abuses.
As unrest multiplies rapidly, cries are heard across the globe.
From heaven above, the Father sees and hears as He probes.

With a heart of compassion and understanding, He draws near.
Those with hearts of understanding, He draws into His sphere.
Breathing upon those with ears to hear, He anoints abundantly.
With a double portion, His anointing pours forth triumphantly.
In a spirit of unity, the anointed ones rise to engage mightily.

∼

But you have an anointing from the Holy One,
and you know all things.

1 John 2:20

Rise of the Anointed Ones
Anointed for Such a Time
40 Days to a Deeper Walk with God

By Kenneth L. Birks

Table of Contents

Anointed for Such a Time	1	Clothed in Humility	93
Sound the Alarm	5	Cultural Deception	97
Discovering Spiritual Gifts	11	Restoring Truth	101
Seasons of Time	15	Bride of Christ Revealed	105
World Gone Wrong	19	Increasing Fervency	111
The End-Time Revival	23	Kingdom Perspectives	115
Cultivating Newness	27	Avoiding Worldliness	119
In Sync with God's Purposes	33	Transformation Process	123
Path of the Righteous	37	Against the Current	127
God's Power: Sword and Spirit	41	Dominant Concerns	131
The Helper of our Joy	45	Flames of Fire	135
Grace That Teaches	49	The Joyful Sound	139
Spiritual Renewal Cost	53	The Antichrist Spirit	143
Cast Your Bread on the Waters	57	Moral Excellence	149
Enduring Shakings	61	God our Stronghold	155
Pursue Peace with All	65	Fortify Your Stronghold	159
Trees of Righteousness	69	Staying the Course	165
Flourish Where You're Planted	73	The Second Coming	169
Word Mixed with Faith	77	About the Author	175
Patterns of Good Works	81	Books and Workbooks	176
Stirring Up Spiritual Gifts	85	Reviews and References	179
The Secret Place – Our Refuge	89	Online Connections	182

Foreword

If there was ever a set of devotionals fit for these times, this is it. In his devotional titled, "Anointed for Such a Time," Ken Birks talks about Mordecai reminding Queen Esther, *"Yet who knows whether you have come to the kingdom for such a time as this?"* Ken's devotional is perfectly fit for a time such as this. As you read through the 40 devotionals, you will find a beautiful blend of timeless truths fitly applied to today's culture and challenges. Ken's insights will challenge you to grow *"in the knowledge of the Son of God and become mature... Then (you) will no longer be infants, tossed back and forth by the waves, and blown here and there by every wind of teaching and by the cunning and craftiness of men in their deceitful scheming." – Ephesians 4*

We live in an age of shallowness and deceitful scheming. I have known Ken for almost 20 years. I have come to realize he has a deep and rich combination of relationship with the Lord, knowledge of the Scripture, and awareness of how truth relates to our present culture. When I went through my own "Dark Night of the Soul," Ken was instrumental in bringing me back to a place of wholeness. As I read through these devotionals, I find much of the wisdom Ken shared with me on that journey.

Each devotional stands on its own, but together they will propel you into a rewarding journey of experiencing God's presence in tumultuous times. I would encourage you to open your Bible and read each devotional with an expectant heart. May you **Get Ready** in these momentous days and experience what it means to rise with the anointed ones. *– Robert Guild, Associate Pastor, Mosaic Christian Church, Rocklin, CA*

Ken's book is like a voice in the wilderness calling God's beloved away from all that distracts to Him who is jealous for His bride. The reader who hears and responds will bring joy to the heart of God and encouragement to others who have put their hand to the plow. *– David Fredrickson, Senior Pastor (Retired), Evangel Christian Fellowship, Sacramento, CA*

Ken Birks has written a masterpiece of superb continuity. The majestic flow from theme to theme contains powerful prophetic revelation, as God calls His end-time warriors to arise. I was also amazed by the poems that followed each devotional – the words were Davidic and musical – they flowed like delightful streams with heavenly impartations. *– Edward Becker, Senior Pastor, Naches Valley Community Church, Yakima, WA*

Day 1

Anointed for Such a Time

There is no doubt we are in the midst of tumultuous times. As we experience one catastrophe after another including a worldwide pandemic, it's obvious. Riots with cities in flames, hurricanes, political unrest, earthquakes, and turmoil amid a world filled with hatred towards those who think differently are all part of what has now become our normalized world. It appears our world is falling apart at its seams. As Christians, what are we to do in an environment that is controlled by violence, fear, and the terror of what is to come? Have we been anointed for such a time as this?

In the book of Esther, we discover Queen Esther, who found herself embroiled in a similar period of unrest when her people, the Jews, were on the verge of being eradicated from the face of the earth. Just as Mordecai suggested that she had come into the kingdom for such a time, so have we. It may very well be that we have been placed strategically where God has planted us for such a time.

Esther 4:24 For if you remain completely silent at this time, relief and deliverance will arise for the Jews from another place, but you and your father's house will perish. Yet who knows whether you have come to the kingdom for such a time as this?"

Let's keep in mind that one of the antichrist's goals will be to eradicate Christians from the face of the earth. Many will fall away during his reign, but God has a plan for His people just as He did for the Jews during Esther's reign as queen. We have been anointed for such a time as this. We cannot afford to remain silent. We must stir the anointing within us and pursue our callings as the Lord gives voice before His great army.

Anointed For Such A Time – Rise of the Anointed Ones

We all have the anointing of the Holy Spirit within us. It is something that God freely gave to us who are in Christ. As we are joined together in unity, His voice will echo throughout the world, providing hope to a world filled with despair.

1 John 2:27a But the anointing which you have received from Him abides in you.

Before this verse, John wrote concerning the coming Antichrist and how the antichrist spirit was already deceiving them as to who Christ was. He reminded them that they had an anointing from the Holy One and knew everything. God is speaking and reminding us once again that we have an anointing within us to stir up and release so that His body is glorified amid all that is happening in our world today. We have been anointed for such a time as this.

> As the Day of the Lord draws near, we must rise as God's anointed ones with one voice as a light amid the darkness, captivating hearts everywhere.

As the Day of the Lord draws near, we are called to rise as God's anointed ones with one voice with a light amid the darkness, captivating hearts everywhere. Through the anointing, we will discover our gifts, talents, and placement in the body of Christ. As He builds us together as lively stones, we will be His light and voice to a world embroiled in catastrophic events.

1 Corinthians 12:4-7 There are diversities of gifts, but the same Spirit. ⁵ There are differences of ministries, but the same Lord. ⁶ And there are diversities of activities, but it is the same God who works all in all. ⁷ But the manifestation of the Spirit is given to each one for the profit of all:

The above passage clarifies to us the Father's purpose and vision. The manifestation of the Spirit is for the purpose of making the anointing within us visible to those without Christ. As we stir the anointing within, we can rise as a powerful entity in the earth amid all the confusion the antichrist spirit is producing. We have been anointed for this season as God manifests His mighty miracle-working power in His Church throughout the earth. The Holy Spirit has ordained His anointed ones for such a time as this to fill the world with the fullness of Him, who fills all in all.[1] May we all prepare to be a part of the "Rise of the Anointed Ones," who go forth as His ambassadors, filling the earth with the Father's glory. May His glory rise upon us as we go into the harvest fields of the earth

---

[1] Ephesians 1:22-23

fulfilling the "Great Commission" to which we have been called to in this hour of the Church's destiny.

Poem: Rise of the Anointed Ones

As storm clouds brew over the land, the earth trembles.
As unrighteousness manifests throughout, evil dissembles.
Troubles coming from every direction, darkness covers.
As anxiety, depression, and fear invade, multitudes suffer.
Engulfed in the madness of the moment, numbness buffers.

Given to the spirit of the times, sinful behavior normalizes.
Blinded by self-absorbed, unrighteous ones; denial demonizes.
Filled with hate and violence, the antichrist spirit abuses.
As unrest multiplies rapidly, cries are heard across the globe.
From heaven above, the Father sees and hears as He probes.

With a heart of compassion and understanding, He draws near.
With hearts of understanding, He draws us into His sphere.
Breathing upon those with ears to hear, He anoints abundantly.
With a double portion, His anointing pours forth triumphantly.
In a spirit of unity, the anointed ones rise to engage mightily.

For such a time as this, His anointed ones soar with eagle wings.
Not growing weary, they run, basking in His glory, overcoming.
In the power of His might, they go as gifts release everywhere.
As the earth fills with His presence, He is known globally.
Throughout the land, His anointed ones are known universally.

The restoration of all things at hand, the anointed one's march.
They come great and strong, the like of whom has never been.
The Lord giving voice, marching perfectly, they recover all.
The earth quaking before them, the unrighteous writhe in pain.
As the heavens tremble, strong is the One who executes.

Prayer

Father God, I come before you today asking for more oil in my lamp. Allow Your anointing to fill my heart with goodness and mercy as I go forth as one of Your vessels of Honor. Open my heart to what You are doing in my field of harvest as I go about my day. Help me to continually stir up the gifts You have given me.

~

Anointed For Such A Time – Rise of the Anointed Ones

May you be blessed in all that you do as you go forth in the anointing of the Holy Spirit.

Day 2

Sound the Alarm! The Day of the Lord is Near

Is God about to do something extraordinary? This is a question to ponder if we desire to be a part of the prophetic fulfillment of the times before the Second Coming of Christ—the Day of the Lord. As the prophet Joel declares, we are to sound the alarm and warn all that the Day of the Lord is at hand. Now is the time to make ourselves ready as His instruments of righteousness.

***Joel 2:1-2** Blow the trumpet in Zion and sound the alarm in My holy mountain! Let all the inhabitants of the land tremble; for the day of the Lord is coming, for it is at hand: ² A Day of darkness and gloominess, a day of clouds and thick darkness, like the morning clouds spread over the mountains.*

In Peter's great sermon following the healing of the lame man at Solomon's Porch in the book Acts, he makes the point that Jesus won't return until the restoration of all things happens, and everything spoken by the mouth of the prophets is fulfilled.[2] The above passage is a prophetic statement concerning the times we are entering. We are at a point in time when our worldly climate demands we make ourselves ready. The trumpet has begun to sound the alarm warning the inhabitants of our world to get prepared for what God is about to do. We are entering into a season of urgency, wherein we must first make sure we clothe ourselves in the Lord Jesus Christ by putting on our wedding garments. Will we be among those who have prepared ourselves for the great wedding day, or will we be caught unaware suddenly when the day comes on us? Preparing ourselves

---

[2] Acts 3:11, 19-21

for how to be used in this season is an important question for all of us to ponder as we prepare for our Lord's Second Coming.

Revelation 19:7 *Let us be glad and rejoice and give Him glory, for the marriage of the Lamb has come, and her wife has made herself ready.*

Romans 13:13-14 *Let us walk properly, as in the day, not in revelry and drunkenness, not in lewdness and lust, not in strife and envy. ¹⁴ But put on the Lord Jesus Christ, and make no provision for the flesh, to fulfill its lusts.*

The trumpet sound emanating from the throne of God is a wake-up call for the Church. We must wake up from our slumber and realize the alarm is sounding. We have a grave responsibility to be watchmen on the walls to warn the world, our friends, and loved ones of the impending disaster that is coming on all the inhabitants of the world, lest their blood is upon us. We must open our hearts and spirits to the alarm sounding throughout the world's landscapes and allow the Holy Spirit to speak in a way we understand. As the prophet Ezekiel warns us, God made us security guards for His house. We are to warn the world's inhabitants to save them from their sins.[3] He says their blood will be upon us if we fail to do so. It is evident; Paul was well versed in the words of Ezekiel. When speaking to the leaders of the church at Ephesus, he said, *"I am innocent of the blood of all men."*[4] During the whole of Paul's ministry, he was motivated to sound the alarm and boldly proclaim the gospel to everyone he met. How motivated are we to sound the alarm to those we meet and know?

To remain in a state of readiness, we need to have the anointing oil flowing from our lives as we commit to His purposes for our generation. Without the anointing, we won't be adequately prepared to minister in the fullness of Christ with the gifts of the Spirit He has given. John informs us in one of his letters that we all have the anointing of God.[5] What are we doing with the anointing God has given us? Are we stirring it up daily? We have been given the power of the Holy Spirit to minister supernaturally to a world filled with hate, violence, sexual depravity, deceit, and much more that exudes out of self-absorbed people caught in the lies of Satan. We are to be salt and light amid a dark and oppressed climate. Through the anointing of the Holy Spirit in the life of Jesus, He was able to penetrate the darkness that assaulted the lives He set free. We have been given that same anointing as the following passage of Scripture reveals.

---

[3] Ezekiel 3:17-20
[4] Acts 20:26
[5] 1 John 2:20, 27

Rise of the Anointed Ones – Sound the Alarm

***1 Corinthians 12:4-7** There are diversities of gifts, but the same Spirit. [5] There are differences of ministries, but the same Lord. [6] and there are diversities of activities, but it is the same God who works all in all. [7] But the manifestation of the Spirit is given to each one for the profit of all.*

The term "works" means active operation, productive, powerful, dynamic, efficient, fervent, and mighty in showing forth. The word "manifestation" means to make visible, clear, and known. With these two definitions in mind, we can see that it is the Father's desire for us to be vigorous and mighty in showing forth and making His power visible through the gifts of the Spirit.

> To remain in a state of readiness, we need to have the anointing oil flowing from our lives as we commit to His purposes for our generation. Without the anointing, we won't be adequately prepared to minister in the fullness of Christ with the gifts of the Spirit He has given.

There is an end-time anointing that is coming before the return of Jesus Christ that will be far greater than anything that has occurred throughout the earth's history. God is now commissioning us to fulfill the words of Jesus when He said, *"You will do greater works than Him."* This anointing will come suddenly like a mighty rushing wind as it did with the early disciples in the book of Acts. So now is the time as Christ's bride to make ourselves ready. As we hear the trumpet sounding the alarm, we must take the time to fill our vessels with the oil of the Holy Spirit as we purpose to go forth in His anointing.

As chaste virgins[6] espoused to Christ, let us not be like the foolish virgins who took no oil with them while they waited for their bridegroom.[7] Instead, let us be like the wise virgins whose lamps were filled and ready to move in step with God's plans and purposes. The prophet Joel also mentions this when he says, *"A people is coming, great and strong, the like of whom has never been nor will there ever be any such after them, even for many successive generations."*[8] The prophet, Daniel, said, *"The people who know their God shall be strong and carry out great exploits. Those who are wise shall shine like the brightness of the firmament, and those who turn many to righteousness like the stars forever and ever."*[9] Therefore, let us heed the words of Paul, the apostle.

---

[6] 2 Corinthians 11:2
[7] Matthew 25:1-10
[8] Joel 2:2b
[9] Daniel 11:32, 12:3

Rise of the Anointed Ones – Sound the Alarm

Romans 14:11-14 *And do this, knowing the time, that now it is high time to awake out of sleep; for now, our salvation is nearer than when we first believed. [12] The night is far spent; the day is at hand. Therefore, let us cast off the works of darkness, and let us put on the armor of light. [13] Let us walk properly, as in the day, not in revelry and drunkenness, not in lewdness and lust, not in strife and envy. [14] But put on the Lord Jesus Christ, and make no provision for the flesh, to fulfill its lusts.*

As the alarm reverberates through our spirits, may we go into our harvest fields, sounding the alarm as God displays His glory. With the rise of the anointed ones, God will usher multitudes upon multitudes into His kingdom before the great and notable day of the Lord.[10] May we not be caught sleeping as this excellent opportunity to be used by the Lord is upon us. The time to get ready is at hand. By preparing to get the extra supply of oil for all that God has prepared for this crucial time in the history of the earth, we will be ready for the second coming of Jesus Christ. May we sound the alarm for all to hear.

Poem: The Day of the Lord

As darkness and oppression take over, alarms begin to sound.
With the Day of the Lord at hand, a voice thunders, "Get ready!"
At the sound of the alarm, inhabitants of the land begin to tremble.
With the alarm reverberating throughout the land, madness rules.
As the voice thunders, alarms go off, captivating all who hear.

Awakened out of spiritual slumber, revelation incites action.
Darkness gripping hearts everywhere, many stand in wonder.
Poised for action, many stand ready with their lamps lit with oil.
With the day of the Lord at hand, a sense of urgency captivates.
Like a mighty rushing wind, His fullness comes to those with oil.

As lamps fill, signs and wonders disarm those caught in madness.
Touched by the anointed ones, hope invades those lost in darkness.
Miracles with great exploits multiplied, the anointed one's minister.
Fulfilling prophetic words from prophets of old, they dispel darkness.
Multitudes in valleys of decision, many turn in repentance.

The sickle put to the harvest; He reaps with an abundance turning.
Spewing venom in anger, Satan knows the Day of the Lord is near.
Those reaped, the Father rescues as Satan spews venom like a flood.
On wings of an eagle, anointed ones escape to a place of refuge.

---

[10] Joel 3:13-15

Nurtured and provided for, they dwell as havoc wreaks everywhere.

No longer restrained, the anointed out of the way, Satan's fury releases.
With power to kill and destroy, the foolish ones without oil, he martyrs.
With power to deceive, usurping God's authority, masses follow blindly.
With the anointed ones taken out of the way, God releases His wrath.
Seven Angels given seven vials; they pour wrath on all inhabitants.

With God's mystery finished, the culmination of all things is at hand.
The fullness of His wrath released; Mighty God signals He's ready.
The Day of the Lord at hand, the Righteous One mounts His Horse.
The dead in Christ risen, the anointed ones are raptured to meet Him.
Gathering His troops from the four corners, they mount up and ride.

With Armageddon as their destination, the Day of the Lord arrives.
The inhabitants destroyed by His brightness; He takes possession.
Setting feet on the Mount of Olives, He's ready to set up His throne.
With Satan, the antichrist, and the false prophet bound, He conquers.
Ruling and reigning a thousand years, the Day of the Lord fulfills.

Prayer

Lord, help me maintain my focus on You and all that you desire to do in my life and those around me. Help me be a diligent watchman and ready to respond to all that comes my way.

~

May you rise with courage in your heart as you purpose to sound the alarm to those in your field of harvest.

Day 3

Discovering Spiritual Gifts

The gifts of the Spirit play a vital part in all that God plans to do through His Church, the body of Christ, before Christ returns for His bride. Therefore, it's important for us to discover the spiritual gifts He has given to each of us. His gifts are a vital part of the person He has created us to be as we fulfill our roles in the end-time harvest of souls.

1 Corinthians 12:7 But the manifestation of the Spirit is given to each one for the profit of all.

Because the gifts of the Spirit play a significant role in the end-time environment, we need to fan the flame by stirring them up. We have all received at least one of the gifts of the Spirit. In his letters to the churches, Paul says God gave gifts for the profit of all. Therefore, God desires that we all discover and use the spiritual gifts He gave us. We will not experience the fullness God has ordained for our lives unless we find, and use the gifts freely given to us by the Holy Spirit. Once discovered, we then begin to fan them into existence by using them regularly.

In Paul's first epistle to the Corinthians, he was concerned that they would not be lacking concerning the gifts of the Holy Spirit as the day of the Lord draws near.[11] His heart towards them was that they would be well used in the gifts of the Holy Spirit, which prompted him to spend ample time explaining their proper usage for the glorification of the body of Christ.

Paul also wrote to Timothy to stir up the gift of God which he received. To stir means to kindle afresh or keep in full flame. Metaphorically, it refers to the fact that the gift of God is like a fire capable of dying out through neglect. In other words, we must continually fan the flames with fresh kindling.

---

[11] 1 Corinthians 1:7

Rise of the Anointed Ones – Discovering Spiritual Gifts

Knowing we have access to the gifts of the Spirit through the Holy Spirit; it is our responsibility to discover them. So then, as the Father distributes His gifts as He wills,[12] He prepares our hearts to receive all we need for the tasks and purposes He has called us to so that we can go forth as His flames of fire filled with His passion.[13]

Discovery is the key that unlocks our spiritual gifts. How do we go about it? There are no simple answers or specific steps. It's a process that comes with our relationship with God the Father through Jesus Christ as the Holy Spirit searches the heart of the Father for those things that concern our lives. He explores the heart of the Father for the spiritual gift or gifts that are best suited for who He created us to be.

1 Corinthians 2:9-10 But as it is written: "Eye has not seen, nor heard, nor have entered into the heart of man the things which God has prepared for those who love Him." [10] *But God has revealed them to us through His Spirit. For the Spirit searches all things, yes, the deep things of God.*

> We will not experience the fullness God has ordained for our lives unless we find out and use the gifts freely given to us by the Holy Spirit. Once discovered, we must then fan them into existence by using them regularly.

Through our relationship with Christ, we begin to discover all that He has created us to be. As we grow and mature in Christ, we catch glimpses of our purpose and ministries. As we begin to grasp who we are in Christ, we think about what gifts of the Spirit would best match our callings. In the letter to the Corinthians, he tells us to desire the best gifts. What are the best gifts? They are the ones that are the best suited for who you are in Christ. The key to fanning the flame for your spiritual gift to burst into an intense love that ministers to others is desire. You must have a sincere desire to be used by God to minister in the gifts of the Spirit.

Once you discover the best gift for who God created you to be, you then begin to press in by learning everything you can about it. Study and seek out others who are well used in it and learn from them. We then step out in faith and start using His gifts. Paul wrote to the Romans, *"Having then gifts differing according to the grace that is given to us, let us use them: if prophecy, let us prophesy in proportion to our faith; or ministry; he who*

---

[12] 1 Corinthians 12:11
[13] Psalm 104:3

teaches, in teaching, he who exhorts, in exhortation; he who leads, with diligence; he who shows mercy, with cheerfulness."

It is of vital importance that we allow God to plant us in local expressions of the body of Christ where we have the liberty to grow and mature in the gifting and ministries to which He calls us to engage. The Church is the body of Christ. It needs its members to function together in unity and harmony with one another for God's glory to manifest in their communities. As each member determines to stir or fan their gifts into flames, we become the flames of fire God has ordained us to be.

Poem: Spiritual Gifts and the Harvest

Chosen by God as peculiar treasures, in Him, we delight.
Distributing gifts to all, He pours into our vessels to ignite.
Given for the profit of all, His body, He desires to glorify.
Given to aid in ministry, we press to receive His best.
Like flames of fire burning with passion, we press to bless.

With the fields of harvest before us, His gifts, we attest.
The word of knowledge at the well, He reaped a harvest.
As prophecies reveal the state of hearts, faith challenges.
With gifts of healings and miracles, crowds gather to hear.
With discerning spirits, demonic strongholds disappear.

Knitted and framed together as lively stones, He builds.
As each stone discovers its gift, He places strategically.
Freely given to expression, we press on, building accordingly.
As each stone freely explores, His glory overshadows.
Bathed in glory, multitudes repent, changing dramatically.

A greater harvest to reap, fully developed, we make ready.
As one body, fully equipped in all gifts, we rise in formation.
Throughout the earth, we go to every tribe and nation.
Fully armed with spiritual weapons, Satan stands aghast.
As Jesus puts the sickle to the harvest, the earth is harvested.

Prayer

Create a desire within me to have a seeking heart to receive all that You have in store for me so that I will be one of Your flames of fire, who ministers to glorify You in everything.

~

May you be filled with the blessings of God as you press into His gifts.

Day 4

Seasons of Time

Throughout the annals of time, seasons have come and gone — some good, some bad. No matter what season we may find ourselves in, God has a purpose to be fulfilled. As born-again, Spirit-filled Christians, we have all been called according to God's purposes, as Paul reminded young Timothy.

2 Timothy 1:9 Who has saved and called us with a holy calling, not according to our works, but according to His own purpose and grace, which was given to us in Christ Jesus before time began.

Just as King David was quoted in Scripture as serving the purpose of God for his generation,[14] God has called us to serve our generation. Therefore, we begin to contemplate how we should respond to His call. Just as the sons of Issachar understood their times and knew what the nation Israel was to do or how they were to respond to their particular season, so should we.[15]

Do we know the nature of the season we are in and how we are to respond to it? Jesus rebuked the Pharisees of His day when He said, *"You know how to discern the face of the sky, but you cannot discern the signs of your time."* Let this not be said of us. As Paul preached, God expects us to be wise and discerning of our times. We are to walk circumspectly in the wisdom God has imparted into our spirits.

Ephesians 5:15-17 See then that you walk circumspectly, not as fools but as wise, [16] redeeming the time because the days are evil. [17] Therefore do not be unwise but understand what the will of the Lord is.

---

[14] Acts 13:36
[15] 1 Chronicles 12:33

Rise of the Anointed Ones – Seasons of Time

Recently, we came through a season where we experienced a worldwide pandemic known as COVID19. If anything, this pandemic opened our eyes to the stark reality that we are in a troubling season. It is a time to thoughtfully consider all that is going on in light of what God's word says about the end time environment. Do we know what time it is? We could very well be in the season the writer of the Book of Hebrews spoke of when he referred to the shaking that is to come before Christ's return.

Hebrews 12:26-29 *whose voice then shook the earth; but now He has promised, saying, "Yet once more I shake not only the earth but also heaven."* [27] *Now this, "Yet once more," indicates the removal of those things that are being shaken, as of things that are made, that the things which cannot be shaken may remain.* [28] *Therefore, since we are receiving a kingdom which cannot be shaken, let us have grace, by which we may serve God acceptably with reverence and godly fear.* [29] *For our God is a consuming fire.*

> Do we know what time it is? We could very well be in the season the writer of the Book of Hebrews spoke of when he referred to the shaking that is to come before Christ's return.

The pandemic shook every aspect of our lives and cultures. It has changed the way we live. God looks down from the heavens above to seek those who understand the times of their seasons. He looks for those seeking Him, who desire to respond to all that's going on in our world.[16] Amid all the turmoil, Jesus is building a Church with His anointed ones to withstand the pressure of these times. He is creating a place of refuge—a strong tower for all of His righteous ones to run into and be safe.[17]

God is looking for those willing to partner with Him as Jesus builds a Church in which the authority of Hell has no power. He plans to remove all that was made according by poorly devised plans through a false self-centered gospel that seeks to appease rather than challenge. Now is the time to rise and build according to the pattern or blueprint shown in Scripture. Paul, the wise master builder, said there is no other foundation than what Jesus laid. He said we are to be careful how we build upon it.

1 Corinthians 3:9-11 *For we are God's fellow workers; you are God's field; you are God's building.* [10] *According to the grace of God, which was given to me, as a wise master builder I have laid the foundation, and another builds on it. But let*

---

[16] Psalm 53:2
[17] Proverbs 18:10

each one take heed how he builds on it. [11] For no other foundation can anyone lay than that which is laid, which is Jesus Christ.

In one of Peter's epistles, he describes us as living stones built up as a spiritual house.[18] We are the strong tower, or the Church Jesus is building of which He desires to fit and frame us as fellow citizens who are being built together as a holy temple. Our part is to yield to the Holy Spirit as He sets and positions us where He specifically designed and created for us.[19]

Only as we seek to discover who we are in Christ and what our gifts, ministries, and callings are can we be fitted together. Allowing the Father to frame us together is the pattern He established to bring forth the glory that will usher in the harvest of souls He has prepared for this season. As we allow the Father to fit and frame us together, it brings forth His glory that fills His temple, the body of Christ, in the same way Solomon's temple was.

Therefore, our responsibility is to lose our "Me Too" attitudes prevalent in today's secular and church cultures. We are to deny ourselves and submit to the process that binds us in unity by submitting to one another in fear of God. We are to speak the truth in love to one another as we grow up in all things into Him who is the head—Christ.

Ephesians 4:16 *from whom the whole body, joined and knit together by what every joint supplies, according to the effective working by which every part does its share, cause growth of the body for the edifying of itself in love.*

What is God is about to do? He is looking for those of His body who have been diligently joining themselves together in unity. Let us not be caught unawares in the season He gave us to sow in. Let us fully embrace our season and serve the purposes of God for our generation.

Poem: Adjusting to Changing Seasons

With changing times, lost in wonder, we question.
Round and round, we go searching for attention.
Lost in a state of confusion, we give into cynicism.
As mania surrounds, fear gives birth to extremism.
Caught in the moment, we look for a connection.

Questioning the absurdity of all, we seek direction.
As peaceful times disappear, we long for solutions.

---

[18] 1 Peter 2:5
[19] 1 Corinthians 12:18

Given to attitudinal changes, hope gives birth to faith.
As fresh winds blow, new fragrances, we sense.
No longer victimized, we turn to the season with faith.

As new fragrances take hold, hearts fill with vision.
Finding purpose and vision faith leads to decisions.
Alive in the Spirit, spiritual authority brings deliverance.
As strongholds dissolve, righteousness spreads rapidly.
Looking down from heaven, the Father smiles heartily.

Prayer

Father God, I look to you today for wisdom and understanding. Help me to be of those You find seeking. I commit my life as a living stone. Fit and frame me into what You desire in this season of my life. Increase my sensitivity to all that You want to do in our world today.

~

May God bless you mightily as you purpose in your heart to fully follow Him no matter what season you may be facing.

Day 5

Becoming Christlike In a World Gone Wrong

Let's face it, as followers of Christ, we now find ourselves trying to navigate in a self-absorbed world gone wrong. Today's world is filled with violence, deceit, sensuality, and every known sin to humankind — sin that is not only accepted by the multitudes but promoted without any sense of shame whatsoever. We live in polarized societies that promote hate and violence to those who disagree with a collective mindset set against Judeo-Christian morals. The challenge for all Christians is to exhibit Christlike morals and attitudes to those caught up in a world gone wrong. The passage below shows how God's word gives us good advice.

Philippians 2:5-7 *Let this mind (attitude-NASB) be in you, which was also in Christ Jesus, ⁶ who, being in the form of God, did not consider it robbery to be equal with God, ⁷ but made Himself of no reputation, taking the form of a bondservant, and coming in the likeness of men.*

Amid all that is going in today's world, how should true disciples of Jesus respond in a world gone wrong? Jesus is our supreme example.

First, we must become increasingly like Christ as the Holy Spirit transforms us from glory to glory. To do this, we must yield to His transforming power.

2 Timothy 2:24-26 *And the servant of the Lord must not quarrel but **be gentle** to all, **able to teach, patient** ²⁵ in humility correcting those who are in opposition, if God perhaps will grant them repentance, so that they may know the truth ²⁶ and that they may come to their senses and escape the snare of the devil, having been taken captive by him to do his will.*

Secondly, we teach, being patient with those who are in opposition to God.

Thirdly, through humility and gentleness, we are to correct those who are in opposition to God and all that He stands for.

These are challenging times for God-fearing Christians. We can get swallowed up in the herd mentality or choose not to get squeezed into a world gone wrong. To avoid the squeeze of the world, we must put on the same garments as our Savior, the Lord Jesus Christ, making no provision for the flesh. The immense pressure to accept conformity to the world will continue to increase as this age ends. Now is the time to arise out of our sleep and clothe ourselves in the Lord Jesus Christ. Our current season demands that we diligently add to our faith the character traits that Jesus exhibited as He walked in this earthly realm as Peter, the Lord's disciple, instructs us.

2 Peter 1:5-11 But also for this very reason, giving all diligence, add to your faith virtue, to virtue knowledge, [6] to knowledge self-control, to self-control perseverance, to perseverance godliness, [7] to godliness brotherly kindness, and to brotherly kindness love. [8] For if these things are yours and abound, you will be neither barren nor unfruitful in the knowledge of our Lord Jesus Christ. [9] For he who lacks these things is shortsighted, even to blindness, and has forgotten that he was cleansed from his old sins. [10] Therefore, brethren, be even more diligent to make your call and election sure, for if you do these things, you will never stumble; [11] for so an entrance will be supplied.

> We live in polarized societies that promote hate and violence to those who disagree with a collective mindset set against Judeo-Christian morals. The challenge for all Christians is to exhibit Christlike attitudes to those caught up in a world gone wrong.

Peter assures us, if we diligently clothe ourselves in the fruit of the Spirit, we won't get squeezed into the world's mode. Instead, we will be fruitful in how the Lord has called us. He calls us to let our lights shine brightly amid a world gone wrong. We are to be a city on a hill. When we spew out venom rather than responding with a spirit of gentleness, our lights are covered and useless. We are the salt of the earth. If our salt loses its flavor due to negative attributes, it is useless and good for nothing. Is this what we want our testimony to be? In a world where sin abounds, the Christian should be infused with an extra supply of grace, as the Word says, *"Where sin abounded, grace abounded much more."*[20]

---

[20] Romans 5:20

We are entering a season where God gives an extra oil supply to those who are pressing in and embracing Christlike attitudes with a desire for a fresh anointing. They receive an increase in their anointing for their lamps to shine brightly amid the spiritual darkness beginning to cover the earth.

***Matthew 25:1-4** Then the kingdom of heaven shall be likened to ten virgins who went out to meet the bridegroom. ² Now five of them were wise, and five were foolish. ³ Those who were foolish took their lamps and took no oil with them, ⁴ but the wise took oil in their vessels.*

As the Scriptures teach us, God has destined us to arise and shine in a darkened world. As a result, many will be drawn to our lights and ushered into the kingdom just as the prophet Isaiah prophesied.

***Isaiah 60:2-3** For behold, the darkness shall cover the earth, and deep darkness the people; but the LORD will arise over you, and His glory will be seen upon you, ³ The Gentiles shall come to your light, and kings to the brightness of your rising.*

Now is the time to prepare for this great harvest season by getting an extra supply of oil. Prophecies concerning the season of darkness are already upon us. This season is a time for faithful followers of Jesus Christ to get serious and walk as children of the light, manifesting the fruit of the Spirit, awakened from our sleep. As we willingly embrace the darkness, Christ will give us light. We have come into the kingdom for such a time as this — being Christlike in a world gone wrong. As we do, it will give rise to the anointed ones shining brightly.

May God bless you as you put on the armor of light by clothing yourselves in the Lord Jesus Christ while making no provision for the flesh.

Poem: Manifesting the Presence of Christ

With a fruitful harvest in mind, the divine seed, He plants.
Planted deep in the earth's crust, it bursts forth in His likeness.
As a grain of wheat has many seeds, His seed multiplies.
Going forth in His likeness, the seed planted bursts forth.
In a powerful display of power, transformation emerges.

Born of the Spirit, His seed planted, hearts begin to produce.
As the seed takes root, new life springs forth bearing leaves.
Watering the seed with the Word, trees of righteousness appear.
As the planting takes shape, fruit bursts forth in abundance.
Faith to faith, spiritual growth is evidenced in Christlikeness.

Making no provision for the flesh, a new nature emerges.
As the new man in Christ emerges, the old disintegrates.
From glory to glory, Christ reveals Himself in those emerging.
Putting on the garments of the new man, the old are tossed.
Adding to the faith, virtue; knowledge produces self-control.

With godliness, kindness, and love in place, newness takes over.
Filled with power and authority, the new man emerges in fullness.
Knitted and joined together in Christlikeness, His body emerges.
Fully surrendered, embracing His cross, His body magnifies.
His seed multiplied; Christ appears in His glory through His body.

With His presence manifested, His Body harvests and gleans.
With signs and wonders filling the harvest fields, they reap.
As multitudes upon multitudes enter, they are transformed.
With many laborers praying into the harvest, much is gleaned.
With the harvest reaped, the coming of the Lord is prepared.

Prayer

Father, in the name of the Lord Jesus Christ, I come to you today offering my heart to you as a sacrificial offering. Take my life and mold it into a vessel of Your righteousness. Help me be a light amid all that is wrong in our world. Help me be a blessing to all those I come in contact with as I go about my day that I might spread salt in a decaying world.

~

May the Lord bless you mightily as you yield to the Holy Spirit and allow His fruit to fill your life in a world gone wrong.

Day 6

The End Time Revival

No matter what season we may find ourselves in, the fields are always white for harvest, as Jesus pointed out to His disciples. Even though harvests have come and gone, there is an end-time harvest coming that will far exceed anything the world has experienced, including the time Jesus was here on the earth and the first 100 years or so following His resurrection.

John 4:35 "*Do you not say, 'There are still four months and then comes the harvest'? Behold, I say to you, lift your eyes and look at the fields, for they are already white for harvest.*"

Do you believe worldwide revival is possible? Try to imagine what it will be like when the Church rises to the glory spoken of by Isaiah, the prophet. Just as God in His sovereignty brought forth the Messiah according to the timing of Daniel's prophecy, He will bring forth the prophetic purpose of a worldwide revival according to His timing. God's people, whom He plants in every city, village, town, and countryside throughout the world, will stand up as the vast army just as Ezekiel prophesied.[21] God will fulfill His prophetic purpose as He breathes on the dry bones prophesied by the prophet, Ezekiel. It will produce a worldwide revival that is yet to come as the Lord in His zeal sends His ministers forth like flames of fire to fulfill His prophetic purposes during this period.

God has remarkable things in store in the coming days amid the darkness that's beginning to cover the earth. Before Christ returns to set up His eternal kingdom, the glory of God will fill all in all—that's every nook and cranny in the earth just as Paul prophesied to the Ephesians.

---

[21] Ezekiel 37:4-10

Rise of the Anointed Ones – The Coming End Time Revival

Ephesians 1:22-23 *And He put all things under His feet and gave Him to be head over all things to the church,* ^{23} *which is His body, the fullness of Him who fills all in all.*

Many revivals have come and gone since Christ's first coming, but there is one last revival yet to come that will be greater than anything the world has ever experienced. A worldwide revival is coming with many waves before the final outpouring of the Spirit fills the world with the glory of God. What the disciples of Jesus experienced was just a foretaste of what will occur in this coming revival. God will give the world a final display of glory, overshadowed by anything that has happened since the beginning of the world. Because He is a just God, the world will have one last opportunity to believe and repent before His Son comes to judge the earth.

The seed of Jesus, which the Father planted in the earth, will come to full maturity as the many-membered body of Christ manifests the fullness of the stature of Christ. Just as the latter rain brought natural harvests to full maturity after the early spring rains to moisten the ground for the seed to be planted, the latter rain of God's Spirit will bring His body to full maturity from the seed that was planted by the death, burial, and resurrection of Christ.

John 12:23-24 *But Jesus answered them, saying, "The hour has come that the Son of Man should be glorified.* ^{24} *"Most assuredly, I say to you, unless a grain of wheat falls into the ground and dies, it remains alone; but if it dies, it produces much grain."*

> God's prophetic purpose will produce a worldwide revival that is yet to come as the Lord in His zeal sends His ministers forth like flames of fire to fulfill His prophetic purposes during this period.

All that Christ did and accomplished during His three and a half years of ministry will pale in comparison to what's ahead. Because the body of Christ will fully manifest His glory, His many-membered body will do more magnificent works than Jesus did. The manifestation of His glory through His body is a primary reason Jesus told His disciples it was expedient for Him to return to heaven. His seed will multiply as He sends His servants in the fullness of His power to every corner of the world, proclaiming the message of the gospel of Jesus Christ. Every tribe and nation will experience the reality of His glory.

When Jesus ministered in the flesh, He came in the fullness of the Spirit that resulted from the Spirit given to Him without measure. It's evident throughout Scripture that the Father's plans and purposes are for His Church to come into the full measure and stature of the fullness of Christ.

The body of Christ will receive the same Spirit without measure. The Book of Ephesians speaks of how Jesus gave the gifts of apostles, prophets, pastors, teachers, and evangelists to the Church so that His many-membered body can come into the same stature of the fullness that Christ exhibited.

***Ephesians 4:11-13** And He Himself gave some to be apostles, some prophets, some evangelists, and some pastors and teachers [12] for the equipping of the saints for the work of the ministry, for the edifying of the body of Christ, [13] till we all come to the unity of the faith and of the knowledge of the Son of God, to a perfect man, to the measure of the stature of the fullness of Christ.*

The Scripture mentioned above is a prophetic promise that states God's will and purpose for His Church. The Church Jesus is building represents the Father in the same way He did through His incarnation. The zeal of the Lord will bring this to pass, just as He fulfilled other predestinated purposes since the beginning of time. He will continue to make His ministers flames of fire, who go forth to fulfill His prophetic purposes as the culmination of this present age ends. Paul also expressed this thought in the first chapter of Ephesians, where it says, *"And He put all things under His feet, and gave Him to be head over all things to the church, which is His body, the fullness of Him who fills all in all."*

The Prophet, Isaiah, also spoke of this fullness when he said, *"Arise, shine; for your light has come! And the glory of Lord is risen upon you. For behold, the darkness shall cover the earth, and deep darkness the people; but the Lord will arise over you, and His glory will be seen upon you. Then you shall see and become radiant, and your heart shall swell with joy because the abundance of the sea shall be turned to you. The wealth of the Gentiles shall come to you."* – Isaiah 60:1-3

To be involved in all the Lord is about to do, we must prepare our hearts. It's essential to make sure our lamps are full of the oil of His Spirit. Because He will suddenly move as He manifests in every nook and cranny throughout the world's landscapes, we need to be fully equipped for this magnificent time of ministry yet to come.

Poem: Revival Fires Ignited

In the fullness of time, He came, setting hearts on fire.
To all, He came, preaching kingdom power and repentance.
To those responding to His message of love, He set on fire.
Filled with holy passion, embracing the cross, they ran to fulfill.
With destinies to fulfill, revival fires spread rapidly everywhere.

Rise of the Anointed Ones – The Coming End Time Revival

From generation to generation, sparks ignited here and there.
As sparks burst into flames, Jesus continued to build His Church.
With the Holy Spirit released, many voices rose to proclaim.
Challenging dead rituals and traditions, they spoke to inspire.
As reformation fires burned, many hearts were set on fire.

With promises from the prophets of old, revival fires ignited.
From the Welsh to Azusa, hearts inflamed, burned brightly.
As Pentecostals engaged with truths restored, many engaged.
Jesus Freaks to Lutherans, Catholics, and others, fires ignited.
The promise to fill all in all, Jesus continues to build His Church.

As glory filled Solomon's temple, His glory fills the Church.
With Christ planted in the earth, a harvest of His likeness comes.
As the prophet spoke, His glory rises upon those who are ready.
Lamps filled with oil, the anointed ones rise in His likeness.
Works greater than Christ's, in His name, into the harvest, they go.

Amid deep darkness, His glory seen, many stand by in awe.
Where hope was nonexistent, He draws many to light that fulfills.
Drawn by the great light, multitudes upon multitudes, He saves.
With great mercy and grace, His loving-kindness extends to all.
With signs and wonders, in the earth and heavens, He showers.

One last display of mighty power, He gives opportunity to all.
As God's joy floods the earth, His presence is known to all.
As revival fires burn, light overcomes the darkness in all corners.
All tribes and nations hearing and seeing, multitudes turn to Him.
As those who were last become first, they bask in His love.

To those with ears, they hear what the Spirit says to the Church.
Now is the time for vessels unto honor to prepare to be ignited.
Now is the time to cast off the works of darkness as light exposes.
Now is the time to get the extra supply of oil that catapults forward.
Now is the time to be sacrificial offerings to the Lord of the harvest.

Prayer

Heavenly Father, fill my vessel with your Holy Ghost fire. I commit my life to You. Make me ready to engage like those from generations past did.

~

May the blessing of God lead you into being a part of this great revival.

Day 7

Cultivating a Spirit of Newness

Let's face it, we all desire new things. They inspire us until the newness begins to wear off. God's desire for our lives is to give us a new heart that constantly springs forth with a sense of newness thrusting us forward into His purposes for our lives. However, it is our responsibility to cultivate our hearts so that we keep the essence of newness alive while engaging in His assignments.

Ezekiel 36:26-27 I will give you a new heart and put a new spirit within you; I will take the heart of stone out of your flesh and give you a heart of flesh. ^{27} I will put My Spirit within you and cause you to walk in My statutes, and you will keep My judgments and do them.

The problem is our hearts constantly get trampled on by the world and its desires along with life's circumstances. We tend to become hardened as a result. Therefore, if we are to remain in a state of freshness with a constant sense of newness, our hearts need to be cultivated daily. We must continually break up the fallow ground of our hearts if we want the seed of newness to produce the desired fruit.

Hosea 10:12 Sow to yourselves righteousness; reap in mercy; break up your fallow ground, for it is time to seek the Lord till He comes and rains righteousness on you.

The word cultivate means to prepare for raising crops, loosen or break up the soil, foster growth, and improve by labor, care, or study. The next verse in Hosea explains why our hearts get hard from being trampled on. It says we partake of the fruit of lies and trust in our ways.[22] The worldly system

---

[22] Hosea 10:13

Rise of the Anointed Ones – Cultivating a Spirit of Newness

of thought is full of lies because the father of all lies, Satan, controls it. Yet, we find ourselves attracted to his lies and ways of thinking by trusting in our ways rather than God's.

In John the Baptist's message to those who came to him for baptism and heard his message, he gave good instruction on cultivating and bearing fruit. When he arrived on the scene, John came with the message, *"Prepare the way for the presence of Jesus."* He came to plow the ground or cultivate it so that those who heard him could prepare for the newness that was about to spring forth for the Nation of Israel and the entire world.[23]

> If we are to remain in a state of freshness with a constant sense of newness, our hearts need to be cultivated daily. We must continually break up the fallow ground of our hearts if we want the seed of newness to produce the desired fruit.

Luke 3:4-6 as it is written in the book of the words of Isaiah the prophet, saying: "The voice of one crying in the wilderness: 'Prepare the way of the LORD, make His paths straight. ⁵ Every valley shall be filled, and every mountain and hill brought low; and the crooked places shall be made straight, and the rough ways made smooth, ⁶ and all flesh shall see the salvation of God.'"

What was the message John used to get their attention? How did he go about cultivating their hearts so that they could hear the message? He began by using shock treatment to get their attention by calling them a brood of vipers.[24] Using shock treatment helped them see their hearts' condition and need for repentance. He was showing them the wretchedness of their sin. Even though we are new creatures in Christ, we change from glory to glory, which means, if we are to maintain a sense of newness, we must continually recognize and repent from the wretchedness of the sin that holds us back from going to the next level of change.

He then began to strip away their protective shields by telling them, *"Do not begin to say to yourselves, 'We have Abraham as our father.' For I say to you that God is able to raise up children to Abraham from these stones."* What is John doing?[25] He's tearing away at everything secure to them. "We're good Jews." "We obey the commandments." "We're God's chosen people." He first attacks their sense of righteousness and belonging in God's sight as to who they are.

---

[23] John 3:16
[24] Luke 3:7
[25] Matthew 3:9

Rise of the Anointed Ones – Cultivating a Spirit of Newness

Many Jews expected that God would deal extremely hard with Gentile sinners in the judgment, but the Jews, the descendants of Abraham, the friends of God, would be safe. John denounces this attitude and removes the presumed security. He strips away their protective shields to identify with their need for a Savior. By stripping away their protective shields, it allowed them to see the actual condition of their hearts. We should ask ourselves, "What kind of protective shields do we have around our hearts that we need to allow God to tear away to reveal our true condition before the Lord?"

If we are to be vessels of honor to whom God desires to use for gathering in His great harvest of souls, we must continually break up the fallow ground of our hearts. John then invokes the fear of God to provoke responses when he says, *"And even now the ax is laid to the root of the trees. Therefore, every tree which does not bear good fruit is cut down and thrown into the fire." So, the people asked him, saying, "What shall we do then?"* [26]

John's message revealed the condition of their hearts and produced a conviction of their genuine need before God. As we take his message to heart, we become sincere in our repentance. The Father is looking for those to whom He can draw unto Jesus, and this can only happen as a person's heart is prepared through brokenness, which paves the way for cultivation.

The Baptist then hits hard on the theme of repentance, introduced earlier in the passage when he said, *"Therefore bear fruits worthy of repentance."* The theme of repentance was also picked up by Peter when the Jews came to him on the Day Pentecost was fully fulfilled.[27] His message to them was, *"Repent therefore and be converted, that your sins may be blotted out, so that times of refreshing may come from the presence of the Lord."*[28]

The Baptist continues to reveal the type of temptations that are common in all walks of life of which repentance is necessary. To those blessed with abundance, his message was to provide.[29] To continue to horde amid needs is a sin that requires repentance. To the tax collectors or those in charge of collecting various fees, his message was to be honest.[30] To soldiers, police officers, and those in places of authority, the message was don't intimidate,

---

[26] Luke 3:9-10
[27] Acts 2:1, 37-39
[28] Acts 3:19
[29] Luke 3:11
[30] Luke 3:13-13

accuse falsely and be content.[31] John's message was simple. There must be a change in the heart – God is about to act – Judgment is coming – And you must have a new life!

What particular temptations in our spheres of life and influence do we deal with continually that cause our hearts to harden through sin? God is calling all of us to repent and turn to Him so that the times of refreshing will come. He desires each of us to experience the wonderful newness that enables us to walk with a sense of enthusiasm and zeal that brings us into the fulfillment of all our hopes and dreams. The words of the apostle Paul express this thought perfectly.

*2 **Corinthians** 7:11 For observe this very thing, that you sorrowed in a godly manner: What diligence it produced in you, what clearing of yourselves, what indignation, what fear, what vehement desire, what zeal, what vindication! In all these things, you proved yourselves to be clear in this matter.*

Therefore, it is expedient we take to heart the message to prepare the way for the presence of the Lord. But, first, we must ask Him, "What areas of my heart have I allowed to become hardened by the pressures of the world and the circumstances of life?" Then we must break up the fallow ground by applying His word to those areas that have become hardened by our sinful ways.

May God bless you as you break up the fallow ground of your heart! You will be blessed and encouraged with a sense of newness as you press into all that He has for you.

Poem: Cultivate Your Heart

Trampled by carnality and worldliness, the heart disengages.
Weighed down by worldly cares, the soil cries for righteousness.
Disillusionment taking over, the heart gives way to confusion.
Cracked and broken, the soil of the ground yearns to be plowed.
With the promise of righteous rain, prayers for rain are heard.

Committed to cultivating fallow ground, repentance is pursued.
Coming as the early rain, His righteousness rains uninhibited.
As righteousness begins to rain, His love softens the ground.
Cracks disappearing, righteousness covering, chains are unbound.
The ground saturated with righteousness, newness emerges.

---

[31] Luke 3:14

Rise of the Anointed Ones – Cultivating a Spirit of Newness

As newness occurs, transformation sprouts with renewed reality.
The ground watered and nurtured, increase gives way to vitality.
With a spirit of joyfulness, the ground gives way to new fruit.
Immersed in wisdom and revelation, a surge of power is felt.
As a downpour of righteousness extends, new fields are plowed.

Coming as the latter rain, covering the earth, His mercy extends.
Made entirely new, cultivated by His Spirit, the anointed rise.
In His fullness, fully matured, the harvest is beautiful and glorious.
The harvest completed, the earth's fruit is excellent and appealing.
Having escaped from worldliness, they stand ready for His return.[32]

Prayer

Thank you, Lord, for transforming my life and breathing on me in such a way that I continually desire more of You. Help me always to rely on Your sufficiency to maintain a sense of newness that keeps me vibrant in your ways and purposes. Cultivate my heart to be ready to receive the seed that gives birth to new things.

~

May you experience God's transforming power as you allow Him to cultivate your heart as He fills you with vitality and fruitfulness.

---

[32] Isaiah 4:2, John 12:23-26, Ephesians 1:22-23

Day 8

In Sync with God's Purposes

The Psalmist David wrote, *"We are fearfully and wonderfully made."* Speaking of God's Great Book, He says, *"all of our days were fashioned or made for us."* He goes on to say, *"How precious also are Your thoughts to me O God!"* As seen below, Jeremiah expands on this thought by relating it to our future and how God desires to work with us.

Jeremiah 29:11 *For I know the thoughts that I think toward you says the Lord, thoughts of peace and not of evil, to give you a future and a hope.*

In essence, God created and designed us to harmonize with His plans and purposes for our lives. God has wired us with our personalities, innate abilities, and spiritual gifts to operate in relationship with His intentions. Paul says, *"We have been saved and called with a holy calling, not according to our works, but according to His purpose and grace, which was given to us in Christ Jesus before time began."*[33]

Upon salvation, we enter the Father's predestinated purposes. When we come into a relationship with our Creator, He destines everything to come together so that we can be in sync with who He created us to be concerning His purposes. In this process, we must continually yield and submit to the work of the Holy Spirit; otherwise, we short-circuit the way He has so skillfully wired us. When we short-circuit His wiring, things don't go right, and our lives end up in a mess. As Paul wrote, *"We must die daily."* Jesus said something remarkably similar. He said, *"If anyone desires to come after Me, let him deny himself, and take up his cross, and follow me. For whoever desires to save his life will lose it, but whoever loses his*

---

[33] 2 Timothy 1:9

life for my sake will find it."[34] If we want to discover the life the Creator of the universe has created for us, this is what we must do.

Getting involved with God's purposes is what keeps us going as He works in us both to will and to do for His good pleasure. When our hearts are fully engaged and consecrated to Him, He works to align us with His sovereign purposes. Engaging with God with consecrated souls enables His sovereignty to meet with our free will and prepare us to be entirely in sync with Him and His sovereign objectives. God is so concerned about this that He continually searches the earth for those individuals whose hearts are fully committed to Him in this manner.

> When we come into a relationship with our Creator, He destines everything to come together so that we can be in sync with who He created us to be concerning His purposes.

Psalm 14:2 *The Lord looks down from heaven upon the children of men to see if there are any who understand, who seek God.*

2 Chronicles 16:9 *For the eyes of the Lord run to and fro throughout the whole earth, to show Himself strong on behalf of those whose heart is loyal to Him.*

Those who seek God and come in sync with Him are like David, who served the purposes of God for His generation. They are like Paul, who said at the end of his life, *"I have fought the good fight and have finished the race."* Will this be your testimony at the end of your life? Or will you be one of those who short-circuited the way God wired you? The choice is yours. No one can make it for you. Many lives will end in ruin because they tried to re-wire His wiring. They'll have excuses just as those who made excuses to Jesus. But as Jesus said, *"Let the dead bury their dead, but you go and preach the kingdom of God."*

Let the encouraging words from the prophet Jeremiah spur you on to seek God and His purpose for your life with all your heart as the verses following the opening passage urge us to do.

Jeremiah 29:12-13 *Then you will call on Me and go and pray to Me and find Me, and I will listen to you.* [13] *And you will seek Me and find Me when you search for Me with all your heart.*

When convinced God's thoughts towards us are precious and wonderful, we can wholeheartedly embrace all that He has destined for us to walk in. We can then abandon ourselves entirely unto Him.

---

[34] Mark 8:35

Poem: In Sync with God's Purposes

Destined to be all that the Father's called us to, we come.
Knowing we're fearfully and wonderfully made, we give praise.
Acquainted with all our ways, He draws us unto Himself.
Wired by God, He designed us to sync with His purposes.
From heaven above, He finds those who understand.

Saved and called, we enter His predestinated purposes.
Yielding to kingdom desires, our vessels, He uses for His glory.
As vision becomes reality, we move in sync with Him.
With divine nature taking root, thoughts conform to His will.
With the mind of Christ, we go in the power of His Spirit.

Coming to trip us up, Satan questions our calling.
Giving into doubt, we short-circuit God's wiring.
Amid turmoil and struggle, we try rewiring what's broken.
Caught up in ill-devised plans, we stumble in darkness.
Getting back in sync, we repent and humble ourselves.

In mercy, He rewires the mess we made of His handiwork.
With the course somewhat altered, we're back on track.
In full acceptance, we realize His thoughts are precious.
With confidence, we press forward into our high calling.
In sync with Him, we die daily, embracing His cross.

Entirely abandoned unto Him, His anointing, He releases.
His Spirit, no longer quenched, He works His good pleasure.
As sovereignty meets free will, we stay in sync with Him.
Looking down from above, He spies us as valuable vessels.
Prepared and re-wired, we go forth with a conquering spirit.

Prayer

Heavenly Father, help me as You work Your will in me to do Your good pleasure. Help me to know Your thoughts toward me are lovely and filled with goodness. Help me fight the good fight of faith as I go forth, fulfilling what's in store for me. Help me follow hard after You in all things as I focus on You.

~

May God bless you richly as you ponder what it means to be in sync with all that He has destined for your life.

Day 9

The Path of the Righteous

To those who choose to respond to the message of the cross, our Father in heaven offers a beautiful path in life to walk on—a path full of the blessings of God with daily benefits. Therefore, it behooves us to discover how to take full advantage of the path of the Righteous.

Proverbs 4:18 *The path of the righteous is like the morning sun, shining ever brighter till the full light of day.*

As we ponder the above Scripture, our first question should be, "Who becomes righteous and what makes them so special?" The righteous ones are those who believe in the Lord Jesus Christ and what He accomplished when He embraced His cross and died for our sins. Paul spells it out quite clearly in his second letter to the Corinthians.

2 Corinthians 5:21 *For He made Him who knew no sin to be sin for us, that we might become the righteousness of God in Him.* ***2 Corinthians 5:21*** *For He made Him who knew no sin to be sin for us, that we might become the righteousness of God in Him.*

As we stand in the perfect righteousness of Jesus rather than our own, we are made perfect. He writes His laws into our hearts and only sees us through Christ's righteousness. The writer of the book of Hebrews clearly states this strategic revelation of the Father's love when he says by one offering, He has perfected forever those who are being sanctified.

Hebrews 10:14-17 *For by one offering He has perfected forever those who are being sanctified.* [15] *But the Holy Spirit also witnesses to us; for after He had said before,* [16] *"This is the covenant that I will make with them after those days, says the LORD: I will put My laws into their hearts, and in their minds, I will write them,"* [17] *then He adds, "Their sins and their lawless deeds I will remember no more..*

Because we are still carnal, while our new nature is in the process of being renewed or transformed, we grow from glory to glory as He sanctifies us.

Rise of the Anointed Ones – The Path of the Righteous

The Father places us at the foot of a path that must be followed for His transforming power to have its full effect in our lives. Unless we embrace the cross that lies there, we will not be allowed to enter. To believe in the Lord Jesus Christ involves embracing the cross. [35]

> Once we commit to this path by embracing the cross, we take on a whole new perspective. He translates us from the kingdom of darkness into the kingdom of light—the kingdom of God.

Matthew 16:24-26 *Then Jesus said to His disciples, "If anyone desires to come after Me, let him deny himself, and take up his cross, and follow Me. [25] For whoever desires to save his life will lose it, but whoever loses his life for My sake will find it. [26] For what profit is it to a man if he gains the whole world and loses his own soul? Or what will a man give in exchange for his soul??*

Righteousness takes hold when we fully embrace the cross with repentance and whole-heartedly follow Him. As James says, *"Faith without works is dead."* Once we commit to this path by embracing the cross, we take on a whole new perspective. He translates us from the kingdom of darkness into the kingdom of light—the kingdom of God.[36] We then begin the transformation process into becoming Christlike in every aspect of our lives. It is on this path that we discover the fullness of joy as He leads us to pleasures forevermore.

Psalms 16:11 *You will show me the path of life; In Your presence is fullness of joy; at Your right hand are pleasures forevermore.j*

If we stay on this path and hold firmly to it, the Holy Spirit continually works within us, transforming us from glory to glory. Even though we may sin and blow it miserably on occasions, we are still righteous. Because we stand in the righteousness of Jesus, we can get up immediately, without guilt, shame, or condemnation, and run into His loving arms.[37] We can come boldly to His throne of grace because of His righteousness working in us.

Hebrews 4:14-16 *Seeing then that we have a great High Priest who has passed through the heavens, Jesus the Son of God, let us hold fast our confession. [15] For we do not have a High Priest who cannot sympathize with our weaknesses, but was in all points tempted as we are, yet without sin. [16] Let us, therefore, come*

---

[35] 2 Corinthians 3:17-18
[36] Colossians 1:13
[37] Proverbs 24:16, Romans 8:1-2

boldly to the throne of grace, that we may obtain mercy and find grace to help in time of need..

Poem: The Path of the Righteous

Drawn to the light shining on the dark soul, we turn in wonder.
What's this light revealing such darkness within, now drawing?
With the light shining so bright comes an intense tugging.
An often-ignored path becoming visible beckons to consider.
Entering with much apprehension, the light calls for surrender.

Stepping into the unknown, newfound peace floods the soul.
As apprehension and fear dissipate, faith and courage unroll.
Filled with delight, pressing forward, anticipation rises.
As enlightenment swells, tasting fruit from the path emerges.
With new discovery birthed, a sense of invincibility surges.

With freedom tasted, pressing on, we follow the light, so awed.
Led to encounter the light's source, the Son of God is revealed.
Upon investigation, a locked gate blocks, begging to be unsealed.
Holding the key, He says, "In Him, we must trust and yield."
Receiving the key, we realize we must now confess Him as Lord.

Speaking with such affection and kindness, our hearts rejoice.
Sensing love washing over, we yield to the warmth of His voice.
Yielding to the key given, we notice several now attached.
"These are the keys to the kingdom for your journey," He indicates.
Speaking of trials, treasures, gifts, and blessings, they unlock.

Going from faith to faith, righteousness reveals in abundance.
Stepping further into the unknown, fear dissipates in wonderment.
With minds filled with revelation, mysteries become more evident.
Destiny filling our minds, in peace and security, we move, yielded.
No longer apprehensive, we delight in the path now revealed.

Darkness once ruling dissipates, giving way to the light now reigning.
Keys given, open treasures, giving insight to trials and hardship.
Spiritual gifts opened with His keys bring forth purpose, so burning.
Awaiting His fullness dispersed, we walk the path, the Son shining.
Like the light of dawn, the path shines brighter with His glory revealing.

Prayer

Heavenly Father, I come before You to give thanksgiving for seeking me out and helping me to find this excellent path. Your path of righteousness exceeds my expectations. Help me never to forget or take all you have provided on this path for granted.

~

May God bless you mightily as you fully embrace the righteousness found in our Savior, the Lord Jesus Christ. May you experience the fullness of joy as you hold firmly to the path of righteousness.

Day 10

God's Power
The Sword of the Spirit

Many Christians don't realize the power they have available to them with God's word, especially when it's plugged into the power source of the Holy Spirit. They're illiterate or ignorant about what they have in their possession. Knowing what a powerful weapon it is, it's of the utmost importance that we learn how to wield this mighty weapon we have at our disposal.

Hebrews 4:12 *For the word of God is living and powerful, and sharper than any two-edged sword, and of joints and marrow, and is a discerner of the thoughts and intents of the heart.*

Ephesians 6:17 *And take the helmet of salvation, and the sword of the Spirit, which is the word of God.*

Referred to as the sword of the Spirit, God's word, for many, lies unused in the arsenal of weapons at their disposal. As a result, many Christians fall prey as the enemy of their faith traps them with his tactics. They stand weakened in faith, not knowing how to wield this mighty sword that can bring all of Satan's tactics and wiles to naught.

When we fail to wield our swords with the wisdom from above, we give in to our own useless and powerless devices. We face an enemy who understands spiritual warfare and how to use it to his advantage. When the Word of God is not alive and active in our hearts, we fall into the rebuke given by the writer of the Book of Hebrews.

He said, *"For though by this time you ought to be teachers, you need someone to teach you again the first principles of the oracles of God; and you have come to need milk and not solid food. For everyone who partakes*

Rise of the Anointed Ones – God's Power, The Sword of the Spirit

only of milk is unskilled in the word of righteousness, for he is a babe."[38] On the other hand, we have the power of the Holy Spirit teaching and instructing us on how to use God's word while becoming skillful in its use. When we know how to wield the sword of the Spirit with expertise, we are invincible in the battles we face as we move forward in ministry and maturity.

Christians everywhere must now pick up this mighty sword that is more powerful and sharper than anything Satan has at his disposal. What makes this sword living and powerful is that God designed it to be plugged into the power source of the Holy Spirit, who is always at work within us. When He baptizes us into the Holy Spirit in the same way the early disciples were, we plug into the power of the Holy Spirit.

> When we fail to wield our swords with the wisdom from above, we give in to our own useless and powerless devices. We face an enemy who understands spiritual warfare and how to use it to his advantage.

Acts 1:8 But you shall receive power when the Holy Spirit has come upon you, and you shall be witnesses to Me in Jerusalem, and in all Judaea and Samaria, and to the end of the earth.

When God baptized the early disciples in the Holy Spirit, they went forth empowered by Him. As they wielded their swords, they astounded the religious authorities of the day, who had no choice but to acknowledge that these unlearned disciples had been with Jesus as they spoke the word of God.

Acts 4:13 Now, when they saw the boldness of Peter and John and perceived they were uneducated and untrained men, they marveled. And they realized they had been with Jesus.

Do people recognize we've been with Jesus when we speak? Many times, when we speak, we're filled with our wisdom rather than the wisdom of God. It is essential we understand that our wisdom and insight must be fueled by the Holy Spirit and the word of God hidden away in our hearts. When Peter spoke on the day of Pentecost, he was filled with the Holy Spirit and the word of God as he quoted verbatim from the Book of Joel. The Word hidden in Peter's heart exploded when the anointing of the Holy Spirit was engaged. It was the power of God in action. The words that came forth from Peter's lips cut to the heart those who heard him. His sword proved to be sharper than any two-edged sword as it pierced to the

---

[38] Hebrews 5:12-13

division of the souls and spirits of those who heard him. Their response was as follows:

Acts 2:37 *Now, when they heard this, they were cut to the heart and said to Peter and the rest of the apostles, "Men and brethren, what must we do to be saved?"*

If we want to see powerful Holy Spirit-fueled revivals in our day, we must commit to filling our hearts and minds with God's word rather than the vain philosophies of the world and watered-down teachings of the Bible. Three thousand souls discovered the wonderful gift of salvation when they heard Peter's preaching of the unadulterated word of God coming from his lips. Imagine what could happen when the Church quits relying on man's wisdom and devices and depends on the purity of God's word with the Holy Spirit empowering us as Peter encouraged us to do.

1 Peter 4:10-11 *As each one has received a gift, minister it to one another, as good stewards of the manifold grace of God. [10] If anyone speaks, let him speak as the oracles of God. If anyone ministers, let him do it as with the ability which God supplies, that in all things God may be glorified through Jesus Christ, to whom belong the glory and the dominion forever and ever. Amen..*

May the blessing of God be upon you as you go forth in the fullness of the Holy Spirit while relying on the word of God that's hidden away in your hearts as you speak as one who has the oracles of God. Let there be an explosion of His anointing as it interacts with His word in your hearts.

1 John 2:20 *But you have an anointing from the Holy One, and you know all things.*

Poem: Wielding the Sword with Expertise

Staring into space, many stumble, ignoring the sword's power.
As the enemy comes to seduce and destroy, they stand humiliated.
Unable to wield a sword with such potential, they stand intimidated.
Like babes, nursing mother's milk, they stand naked before their enemy.
What will it take to pick up this powerful weapon and use it, they muse?

Tired and worn down from the enemy's tactics, what to do is considered.
Hearing God's word is sharper than a two-edged sword; they're tempted.
Pondering whether to pick it up or let it lie, they consider where to begin.
How to train hands for war, putting the enemy to flight, they ponder.
Having begun in the Spirit, asking for wisdom, they're drawn to its power.

Line upon line, here a little, there a little, it begs to be assessed.
As honey touches the lips, the soul longs to be nurtured and caressed.

With words fitly spoken, His word fills with wisdom from above.
As the Spirit guides through the pages, their minds are renewed.
As present truth establishes, new strength with confidence exudes.

No longer intimidated, swords drawn, they cut asunder.
Words of wisdom flowing freely, his tactics no longer plunder.
Wisdom from above filling heart and mind, the sword sharpens.
Without truth, nowhere to stand, truth slays Satan's empty insults.
Sharper than two-edged swords, Word and Spirit slay as they consult.

Prayer

Heavenly Father, I ask that you give me a heart like David, who loved Your word and what it could do for him. Help me to pick up my sword daily as I hide its contents away in my heart. Help me never take it for granted. Give me the heart to study to show myself approved as a skilled swordsman who is unafraid of the enemy's devices.

~

May you become mighty in God as you learn to wield the sword of the Spirit with expertise.

Day 11

The Helper of Our Joy

It can sometimes seem overwhelming when we think and meditate on all God has called us to do. However, it's essential to remember we have an excellent helper in the universe at our disposal. As we are faithful to ask Him for help, He is always there, ready, and willing to give us the assistance needed. As we utilize the Helper, He lightens our load and provides us with the faith to move forward in all that God has purposed for us. He will never leave us nor forsake us.

*Hebrews 13:6 So we may **boldly say:** "The LORD is my helper; I will not fear. What can man do to me?"What can man do to me?"?"*

What an incredible statement—*"The Lord is my helper!"* Yet many of us continue with our daily lives as if He's nowhere around. We are so accustomed to doing things our way and figuring things out on our own that we forget we have a helper who is on call 24/7.

How many of us are ashamed to call a friend for help when we're involved in a project because we don't want to expose our ignorance? We mess things up because of our pride, thinking we can do it without help. The truth is many have messed up lives because of their stubbornness. They haven't learned to boldly say or confess, "The Lord is my helper."

The reason we can boldly say, "The Lord is my Helper," is that the verse before the above Scripture says, *"I will never leave you nor forsake you."* In other words, the Holy Spirit is continually on call. He is our assistant to help us in all things that pertain to life and godliness.[39] Jesus gave us the tremendous promise that the Holy Spirit would come into our lives as a helper. He said it would be to our advantage.

---

[39] 1 Peter 1:3

Rise of the Anointed Ones – The Helper of our Joy

John 16:7 *Nevertheless, I tell you the truth. It is to your advantage that I go away; for if I do not go away, the Helper will not come to you; but if I depart, I will send Him to you..*

In this world and especially during trying times, we need all the advantages from the Holy Spirit we can get. Therefore, we must boldly proclaim Him as our helper in all things, even in the mundane things of life. By declaring Him as our helper, we learn to lean on Him rather than our ways and methods of doing things. By acknowledging Him as our helper, we fulfill the words of Paul, when he said, "We can do all things through Christ who strengthens me."[40]

The primary key to experiencing the advantage of having a personal assistant on call 24/7 is learning to acknowledge the Lord in all our ways.

Proverbs 3:5-7 *Trust in the LORD with all your heart and lean not on your own understanding;* [6] ***In all your ways acknowledge Him****, and He shall direct your paths.* [7] ***Do not be wise in your own eyes;*** *fear the LORD and depart from evil.*

We need to understand that God's thoughts and ways are so much higher than ours. He views our lives from an eternal perspective that involves our past, present, and future. We may not fully understand why He leads us in specific directions at times because, for the most part, what we see is based on our current circumstances. However, He knows our future and often directs our lives from that perspective. From our carnal perspectives, what may seem like foolishness is the wisdom and the help He desires to give us. Therefore, we shouldn't be wise in our own eyes by ignoring the support He's made so readily available to us through the Holy Spirit, our assistant. We must trust in Him with all our hearts by not leaning on our understanding as we acknowledge Him in all our ways.

> What an incredible statement—"The Lord is my helper!" Yet many of us continue with our daily lives as if He's nowhere around. We are so accustomed to doing things our way and figuring things out on our own that we forget we have a helper who is on call 24/7.

Isaiah 55:9 *For as the heavens are higher than the earth, so are My ways higher than your ways, and My thoughts than your thoughts.*

As we are faithful to commit every day to Him, we openly acknowledge Him in all our ways. By committing our courses to Him, He faithfully

---

[40] Philippians 4:13

establishes our thoughts per His thoughts and wisdom. Committing our thoughts to Him releases the Holy Spirit to be our helper, giving us the advantage as we go about whatever our days may hold.

Proverbs 16:2-3, 9 *All the ways of a man are pure in his own eyes, but the LORD weighs the spirits. ² Commit your works to the LORD, and your thoughts will be established. ⁹ A man's heart plans his way, But the LORD directs his steps..*

Paul said, *"I believed, and therefore I spoke."*[41] Let us do likewise. May we all boldly speak and proclaim, "The Lord is our Helper," as He gives us the advantage in all things that pertain to life and godliness with a testimony that says, *"We can do all things in Christ."* Paul said, *"I believed, and therefore I spoke."* Let us do likewise. May we all boldly speak and proclaim, "The Lord is our Helper," as He gives us the advantage in all things that pertain to life and godliness with a testimony that says, *"We can do all things in Christ."*

Poem: The Helper

Trapped in ideological thoughts swirling about, we question.
Looking for answers, wise in our ways, we forge ahead.
Coming up empty, lost in confusion, we seek wisdom and help.
Calling on the Helper, responding readily, He helps as needed.
Reminding us, He's never left nor forsaken us; he speaks softly.

Ready and willing, He comes with wisdom and understanding.
Taking us by the hand, showing the path, He instructs.
Filled with confidence and assurance, we press forward to gain.
Acknowledging Him in all our ways, He teaches us to trust.
Not putting confidence in self, we relinquish all authority to Him.

Intimately acquainted with our futures, He guides unswervingly.
Instructing to rely on Him as our Helper daily, He speaks.
Knowing He never leaves nor forsakes us, we speak boldly.
Confidently in all things, He's proclaimed as our Helper.
No longer lost in confusion, we trust Him as our assistant.

When circumstances of life pull down, He's there to pull up.
With just a touch He plants our feet on solid ground.
From His eternal perspective, He fills the mind with vision.

---

[41] 2 Corinthians 4:13

Rise of the Anointed Ones – The Helper of our Joy

Raised, seated next to Christ, He shows eternal riches.
From His perspective, seated beside Christ, He comforts.

With the mind set on those things above, He relieves the weight.
The eternal weight of glory glimpsed; we no longer lose heart.
With our thoughts in sync with His, our Helper strengthens daily.
Knowing that we have such a Helper, we can now do all things.
With the advantage given, we're more than conquerors in Christ.

Prayer

Thank you, Heavenly Father, for releasing Your Holy Spirit into my life. I receive Him as the helper of my joy. Amid the circumstances of life that tend to weigh down at times, help me always draw strength from the help He provides. Help me to lean upon Your sufficiency rather than my strength.

~

May you experience the Lord's anointing on every aspect of your life as you call upon Him to be your helper in all things.

Day 12

Grace That Teaches

Most of us understand God saved us by grace, which is the beginning of our walk with Him. But how many of us realize we need God's grace for every aspect of our lives. God designed His grace to abound towards us in all things, while instructing us as we journey through this life as pilgrims.

2 Corinthians 9:8 And God is able to make all grace abound toward you, that you, always having all sufficiency in all things, may have an abundance for every good work.

Titus 2:11-14 For the grace of God that brings salvation has appeared to all men, [12] teaching us that, denying ungodliness and worldly lusts, we should live soberly, righteously, and godly in the present age, [13] looking for the blessed hope, and glorious appearing of our great God and Savior Jesus Christ, [14] who gave Himself for us, that He might redeem us from every lawless deed and purify for Himself His own special people, zealous for good works.

There are several things in the above passages that mention what the grace of God teaches us. First, let's refresh our minds with the fact that God pours His grace into our lives freely based on the righteousness of Jesus Christ rather than our righteousness. There's nothing more we can do to earn more of God's favor. Based on Christ's finished work on the cross, we already have it. All we must do is believe in what He accomplished on our behalf. He became sin for us that we may experience His complete righteousness.[42] Therefore, we have grace abounding towards us for everything that touches our lives.

As we begin to walk in His perfect righteousness, the Holy Spirit, who is now a functional part of our lives, begins to quicken our mortal bodies as

---

[42] 2 Corinthians 5:21

to how destructive our sinful habits are towards the person, He created us to be. His grace now teaches us to deny ungodliness and worldly lusts and live soberly and righteous in this present age, as Paul also wrote to the Romans.

***Romans 6:1-2** What shall we say then? Shall we continue in sin that grace may abound? Certainly not! How shall we who died to sin live any longer in it??*

The grace of God also teaches us to be zealous for good works, which is why Paul urged Titus to remind those who are believers to be careful to maintain good works.

***Titus 3:8** This is a faithful saying, and these things I want you to affirm constantly, that those who have believed in God should be careful to maintain good works. These things are good and profitable to men.*

***Titus 3:14** And let our people also learn to maintain good works, to meet urgent needs, that they may not be unfruitful.*

> How many of us realize we need God's grace for every aspect of our lives? God designed His grace to abound towards us in all things, while instructing us as we journey through this life as pilgrims.

As we are obedient to step out in faith in whatever avenue of good works the Lord is leading, we experience His anointing working in and through us. As we do, His grace teaches and instructs us. As a result, He continually inspires us to be zealous for good works. Stepping out in faith not only increases our divine abilities in Christ but brings us into more of an intimacy with Him as we learn to live and move in the anointing.

Poem: Grace that Teaches

Becoming righteous in Him, we lean into Him, who teaches.
No longer leaning on the arm of flesh, we trust in His grace.
Redeemed from lawless deeds, He purifies as His Own.
A chosen generation, and a peculiar people, He teaches.
As the Cornerstone, He builds us together as living stones.

Teaching us to deny worldly lusts, we live soberly in His sight.
No longer bound with chains of bondage, we're set free.
Loosed from the devil's hold, His grace teaches freedom.
No longer using liberty for fleshly appetites, we freely submit.
Tasting His graciousness, we desire His milk to grow in grace.

Setting our sights on His coming, His grace teaches hope.
No longer bogged down in depression, we hope in Him.

With burdens lifted, He takes us by the hand, leading us.
The eternal weight of His glory before us, He imparts faith.
Showing us wonders of His grace to come, we glorify Him.

Filled with faith and assurance, He teaches us to be zealous.
Zealous for good works, He imparts grace for works ahead.
Divine abilities imparted; grace reveals abilities unknown.
His divine nature taking root, grace is unlimited in all done.
Experiencing unlimited grace in all, hearts fill with His zeal.

Prayer

Heavenly Father, as my heart fills with Your grace, allow it to teach me all that You desire to bring forth in my life. Help me live soberly in Your sight, resting the hope of Your salvation. Allow Your eternal weight of glory to impart faith to my life.

~

May God bless you richly as you allow His grace to teach you in all three of these areas, denying ungodliness and worldly lusts, keeping your focus on His glorious appearing, and being zealous for good works.

Day 13

Spiritual Renewal At What Cost?

No matter who we are, we all need spiritual renewal from time to time. Life can be difficult and pull us under at times. Amid difficulties, we can find ourselves grasping for new waves of spiritual renewal. However, we often discover that our need for renewal can sometimes demand hard work before it fully manifests. It doesn't matter how much emotional pain and turmoil we may experience or how apathetic we may feel, the solution is not always easy. The writer of Hebrews expresses this thought clearly and what we must do to achieve the renewal that is needed before we can go forward into what He has called us to do.

Hebrews 12:12-13 *Therefore strengthen the hands which hang down, and the feeble knees, [13] and make straight paths for your feet, so that what is lame may not be dislocated, but rather be healed.*

Entering spiritual therapy is similar to what a person experiences when beginning physical therapy after an injury or surgery. To recover fully, they must embrace the pain required in physical therapy by doing the hard things or exercises that will put them on their way to complete recovery. The same is true for spiritual recovery. If we desire our soul to be well so that it experiences spiritual renewal, we must be willing to face the painful truth of what's causing our emotional pain and discomfort. To do so involves peeling the protective scabs away to expose the painful wounds. We must honestly, take a hard look at the injuries, thus initiating the process. In the same way, David was proactive regarding self-examination, so must we be. His testimony is as follows:

Psalms 139:23-24 *Search me, O God, and know my heart; try me, and know my anxieties, [24] and see if there is any wicked way in me and lead me in the way everlasting..*

Rise of the Anointed Ones – Spiritual Renewal at What Cost?

Our tendencies are to blame-shift our problems away to ease the guilt, but the problem with blame-shifting is, it doesn't bring spiritual renewal. It just causes the wound to fester until it becomes a root of bitterness. There are no quick fixes. It takes more than prayer, although that's where it begins as it was with David. We live in a world where everything is instant, and if it doesn't come fast enough, we move on to the next thing, hoping for a quick fix. God's ways often require the fruit of the Spirit, patience, while diligently pursuing whatever it takes to experience the renewal we desire. His ways require making straight paths for our feet and doing the hard things for our healing to manifest itself, knowing that God is faithful and true to His word.

Entering spiritual therapy is similar to what a person experiences when beginning physical therapy after an injury or surgery. To recover fully, they must embrace the pain required in physical therapy by doing the hard things or exercises that will put them on their way to complete recovery. The same is true for spiritual recovery.

Hebrews 6:11-12 *And we desire that each one of you show the same diligence to the full assurance of hope until the end, [12] that you do not become sluggish, but imitate those who through faith and patience inherit the promises.*

As the Holy Spirit faithfully searches out the Father's heart towards us, He reveals the paths of healing needed to bring about a renewal in the Spirit that comes as a breath of freshness washing over our souls.

I Corinthians 2:9-10 *But as it is written: "Eye has not seen, nor ear heard, nor have entered into the heart of man the things which God has prepared for those who love Him." [10] But God has revealed them to us through His Spirit. For the Spirit searches all things, yes, the deep things of God."."*

Allowing the Holy Spirit free access to the wounds as He searches the Father's heart concerning our lives is called ongoing repentance. Repentance is much more than forsaking our sins. The basic meaning is conforming our thoughts to God's. As we do, He puts us on track to be molded into the image of Christ from glory to glory. As a result, we continually receive the refreshment from the Lord that keeps us in a state of spiritual renewal. Notice in the following Scripture where it says, *"times of refreshing."*

Acts 3:19 *Repent therefore and be converted that your sins may be blotted out, so that **times of refreshing** may come from the presence of the Lord.*

Repentance and conversion are part of a life-long journey for those of us who have been perfected forever and are continually being sanctified and made whole.

Poem: **Renewal for Beleaguered Souls**

Engulfed in a dry season, stranded in agony, we grope.
Trapped in pain and despair, we cling to a thread of hope.
Snared in a web of hopelessness and weakness, we bemoan.
Stung by loss of faith that once moved mountains, we groan.
Stagnated in a pool of regret, filled with sorrow, we cope.

Facing difficult solutions, we cling to a thread of hope.
Recognizing the need for renewal, our souls cry for mercy.
Hearing the cry of the heart, the Father releases sympathy.
In compassion and mercy, He touches areas infected much.
Touched by His love, our hearts awaken to His gentle touch.

With courage, hands lifted, we embrace renewed activity.
As faith rises, we make decisions for productivity.
Captivity left behind; vision fills the heart with hope.
No longer bound by self-pity, faith rises for challenges ahead.
Necessary faith steps taken, immersed in His Spirit, we tread.

From faith to faith, His righteousness revealed, invincibility occurs.
With renewal fully released, our hearts fully awakened, He restores.
In the might of His Spirit, gifts release for serving and ministry.
With our place at the table restored, peace and joy replace despair.
Giving thanksgiving and praise for His gentle touch, we rejoice.

Prayer

Father, give me strength as I present my body as a living sacrifice to You. Help me make straight paths for my feet while You continually heal and set me free from those areas that hinder me from running the race.

~

May your spirit, soul, and body be renewed as you give yourself to the Lord's therapy, whatever that may be for you.

Day 14

Cast Your Bread Upon the Waters

God, in His word, has given us many wonderful promises that encompass everything needed for our lives.[43] Jesus promised that if we are faithful to seek the kingdom of God first, all things concerning life, such as our food, clothing, and shelter, would be added unto us.[44] As we are faithful to cast our bread upon the waters, it will return just as the preacher said.

Ecclesiastes 11:1 Cast your bread upon the waters, for you will find it after many days.

The degree to which we receive the beautiful blessings of God is dependent upon the law of sowing and reaping. As we are faithful to cast our bread upon the waters, no matter what circumstances we may find ourselves in, God is faithful to cause it to return, especially during times of extreme need.

2 Corinthians 9:6 But this I say: He who sows sparingly will also reap sparingly, and he who sows bountifully will also reap bountifully.

The above scripture outlines the importance of giving, which involves every aspect of our lives including our finances. The more we give of ourselves in every aspect of our lives, the more we will have what we need daily. As it has been said over and over, 'We can't out-give God.' Jesus said, *"Give, and it will be given to you: good measure, pressed down,*

---

[43] 2 Peter 1:2-4
[44] Matthew 6-31-33

shaken together, and running over will be put into your bosom. For with the same measure that you use, it will be measured back to you."[45]

When considering the aspect of giving, we must consider the tithe and why it is essential. Giving of the tithe is a necessary principle for sowing sparingly or bountifully. The promise given for the tithe is similar to the same type of biblical return that Jesus mentioned. It may not be a law, but whether you believe in the giving of the tithe or not, it is a biblical principle of giving and blessing that embraces the principle of sowing and reaping or casting your bread upon the water. The prophet Malachi is quoted as saying, *"'Bring all the tithes into the storehouse, that there may be food in my house, and try Me now in this,' says the Lord of hosts, 'If I will not open for you the windows of heaven and pour out for you such blessing that there won't be room enough to receive it.'"[46]*

Giving the tithe allows us to give systematically so that we establish spiritual disciplines and patterns, which enables God to freely pour His blessings into our lives. It allows the principle of sowing and reaping to affect our lives fully. As the scripture says, *"He daily loads us with benefits."[47]*

I have been a faithful giver of tithes and offerings all my Christian life, encompassing over 50 years. I have many testimonies of how God has blessed our family through the years. Even during transitions when extra income was needed, we were blessed tremendously. For example, during a recent quarantine time because of COVID, we had a stress-free, relaxing, and peaceable time because God's faithfulness allowed us to reap what we had sown. God is good. We have been highly blessed time and time again during our 44 years of marriage. I attribute His blessings to the fact that we have faithfully tithed and given our lives and finances to kingdom purposes while developing a pattern of systematic giving. God has

> The degree to which we receive the beautiful blessings of God is dependent upon the law of sowing and reaping. As we are faithful to cast our bread upon the waters, no matter what circumstances we may find ourselves in, God is faithful to cause it to return, especially during times of extreme need.

---

[45] Luke 6:38
[46] Malachi 3:10
[47] Psalm 68:19

faithfully allowed us to find it when needed as we have been faithful to cast our bread upon the waters.

Casting our bread upon the water is much more than giving our finances. It involves our body, soul, and spirit as it touches every aspect of our lives, including our ministries, family life, work, play, and anything else. In John's third epistle, he reminds us, *"Beloved, I pray that you prosper and be in health, just as your soul prospers."* God desires to make His grace or divine abilities abound towards us in everything our lives touch. If we sow sparingly through self-centered ways, we won't reap the number of blessings He desires to flow in and through us. However, as we commit ourselves to be conduits of His blessings, we can sow and reap bountifully. He aims to fill us with revelation and understanding of who we are in Christ and how He desires to move in our lives with what He's called us to be and do. He has much to give concerning our inheritance in Him.[48] His desire is for us to be partakers of the divine nature that's in Him. God delights in pouring an abundance of grace in us to reap the fullness of all that encompasses our destiny and purpose in Him.

2 Corinthians 9:8-9 And God is able to make all grace abound toward you, that you, always having all sufficiency in all things, have an abundance for every good work. ⁹ As it is written: "He has dispersed abroad; He has given to the poor; His righteousness remains forever."

According to Peter's epistle, the promise involves being partakers of God's divine nature, which gives us everything needed as we minister one to another in the Spirit.[49] Receiving from Him, He pours out of us from His abundance as we involve ourselves in His kingdom purposes. We become conduits of blessing as we sow into the lives of others.

2 Corinthians 9:10-11 Now may He who supplies seed to the sower, and bread for food, supply and multiply the seed you have sown and increase the fruits of your righteousness, ¹¹ while you are enriched in everything for all liberality, which causes thanksgiving through us to God.

Poem: Sowing and Reaping with Joy

Laying treasures before His feet, we give with hearts of fire.
As He multiplies what's sown, we readily engage in His desires.
All things coming from above, we give freely to Him, who owns all.

---

[48] Ephesians 1:17-19
[49] 2 Peter 1:2-4

Of His own, we freely give to Him, acknowledging His ownership.
Freely given, freely received, His blessings in abundance equip.

As revelation and insight take hold, we're conveyed to His sphere.
As transformation enlightens, self-centered ways disappear.
Given new understanding, change affects everything we hold dear.
No longer weighed down, we freely give generously by choice.
Giving generously from what's sown into our hearts, we rejoice.

Enriched for liberality, we give, enabling others to give and receive.
As one sows and others receive, He's glorified as His body believes.
Having sufficiency in all things, we minister with zeal and purpose.
Feeding upon His faithfulness, His grace abounds in service.
From faith to faith, His righteousness, He reveals in abundance.

Involved in His kingdom's purposes, He pours from His treasures.
As our treasures become His treasures, we reap beyond measure.
Filled with His divine nature, we sow abundantly of His treasures.
Into the fields of harvest, we go sowing and reaping joyfully.
Giving of ourselves from His resources, we plant and grow easily.

Joyful in all things, whether abasing or abounding, we sow readily.
Having experienced the abundance of His grace, we plow steadily.
As the fruits of our righteousness increase, we overflow with joy.
Reaping a harvest of righteousness, with thanksgiving, we abound.
As seed multiplies, giving liberally with joyful hearts, we're crowned.

Prayer

As I give unto You and Your kingdom needs, I give myself to You as a conduit to bless others. Therefore, help me be faithful with all You have poured into my life.

~

May the blessings of God be upon your life as you sow and reap with His kingdom's purposes in mind.

Day 15

Enduring Shakings

Our world today seems to be shaking at the seams. Much of what Biblical era prophets prophesied concerning the end-time climate is happening right before our eyes. Considering what's happening in our chaotic world today, we must turn our ears away from the many voices caught in the chaos. With our world shaking in every conceivable arena, we must engage with the Heavenly voice for our spiritual senses to fully awaken with a response that glorifies God in all we do and say..

Hebrews 12:25-29 See that you do not refuse Him who speaks. For if they did not escape who refused Him who spoke on earth, much more shall we not escape if we turn away from Him who speaks from heaven, [26] whose voice then shook the earth; **but now He has promised, saying, "Yet once more I shake not only the earth but also heaven."** *[27] Now this, "Yet once more," indicates the removal of those things that are being shaken, as of things that are made, that the things which cannot be shaken may remain. [28] Therefore, since we are receiving a kingdom which cannot be shaken, let us have grace, by which we may serve God acceptably with reverence and godly fear. [29] For our God is a consuming fire..*

From the pandemic to political unrest, rioting, cities on fire, looting, joblessness, fear, death, persecution, inflation, and more, our world is shaking. Yet, whether all of this fulfills the above prophetic statement or not, the purpose of shaking stands true no matter the degree of shaking we experience. Therefore, now is the time to engage with our ears turned towards the heavenly voice, who gives hope and assurance during seasons of shaking.

The above Scripture most likely speaks of the cataclysmic events that must happen before the return of Christ, but the principle holds true no matter what degree of shaking we may experience. The purpose of shaking is to remove those things that must be destroyed so that the kingdom authority from above rules in our lives. Therefore, we must open our hearts to God's heavenly voice as shakings continue to increase in the days before the second coming of Christ. In doing so, the kingdom of God will not only emerge in our hearts and minds to a greater degree but will bring forth greater blessing to those in our harvest fields where we minister.

By recognizing the seasons of time, we have the choice to prepare ourselves for all that is to come. Our roots need to go deep into the Lordship of our King, the Lord Jesus Christ. As we give ourselves wholeheartedly in obedience to Him and His word, the Holy Spirit who searches the heart of the Father speaks into our lives, so that He may be glorified.

John 16:12-14 *I still have many things to say to you, but you cannot bear them now.* *[13] However, when He, the Spirit of truth, has come, He will guide you into all truth; for He will not speak on His own authority, but whatever He hears He will speak, and He will tell you things to come.* *[14] He will glorify Me, for He will take of what is Mine and declare it to you..*

With each shaking, no matter what it is, when we lean upon God rather than our understanding, a more significant measure of His kingdom's influence is imparted into our lives. The more we allow the Holy Spirit to take what belongs to Jesus and declare it to us, the more stable we become, even during intense times of shaking. When we invest our lives in the kingdom of God, we become unshakeable. We have a terrific opportunity before us to gain experience to run with the footmen before the pace increases..

> With our world shaking in every conceivable arena, we must engage with the Heavenly voice so that our spiritual senses fully awaken with a response that glorifies God in all we do and say.

Jeremiah 12:5 *If you have run with the footmen, and they have wearied you, then how will you contend with horses? And in the land of peace, in which you trusted, they wearied you, then how will you do in the floodplain of the Jordan?*

Poem: The Voice That Thunders

Speaking from the heavens above, His voice thunders.
Awakened to the reality of chaos that surrounds, we ponder.
As thunder explodes at the sound of His voice, we give ear.
Knowing others who did not escape His thunder, we take heed.
With His kingdom emerging at the sound, we follow His lead.

As His voice thunders and shakes, He removes what offends.
No longer attached to all that offends, we stand in reverence.
Giving ear, we stand ready in godly fear to serve in deference.

Rise of the Anointed Ones – Enduring Shakings

With the removal of offenses, hearts no longer clutter.
Experiencing the kingdom within taking shape, we press.

As thunder transforms to joyful sounds, all shakings, we embrace.
Knowing shakings produce greater deposits of grace, we rejoice.
As kingdom authority takes root, stability arrives with assurance.
Ready to run with the horsemen, we stand prepared as He thunders.
Taking charge, we're no longer engulfed in fear of chaos that covers.

With unseen authority as a guiding light, we follow vigorously.
As the heavenly voice thunders, we move in sync as His great army.
Those hearing, march perfectly as His voice thunders vehemently.
With lives fully invested in Kingdom authority, we press on savagely.
As Satan's domains crumble, we recover all, now fully restored.

With great exploits, we press on to a kingdom fully restored.
The Garden of Eden before us, we run, leaving chaos behind.
Like flames fire that devour, nothing escaping, we run to gain.
As His voice thunders, we execute His word, all is obtained.
The earth quaking, heavens trembling, stars diminishing, we reign.

Prayer

Heavenly Father, I open my heart to You in such a way to hear all You have to say concerning how I should respond. Use me to influence others during times of stress and shaking. Keep me sensitive to the voice of Your Holy Spirit in all things.

~

Though your world may tremble and shake at times, may you stand fast in all that comes your way.

Day 16

Pursue Peace with All

One of the Father's greatest desires for His people is for us to dwell in unity with one another. As the Scripture says, *"How good and how pleasant it is for brethren to dwell together in unity."*[50] It will produce an anointing that overflows into the world, causing multitudes to come to salvation in Jesus Christ. For this reason, we are to pursue peace with all peoples.

Hebrews 12:14-15 *Pursue peace with all people, and holiness, without which no one will see the Lord: looking carefully lest anyone fall short of the grace of God; [15] lest any root of bitterness springing up cause trouble, and by this many become defiled..*

The political and social climates in today's world make it difficult to follow the appeal the writer of the above Scripture gives us. However, we must remain peaceable under all circumstances, especially with our Christian brothers and sisters.[51] As followers of Christ, we cannot afford to get caught up in the root of bitterness that's sweeping over the landscapes of our world; let's keep in mind that all Scripture is inspired by God, including the above. It's part of our instruction in righteousness.

2 Timothy 3:16-17 *All Scripture is given by inspiration of God and is profitable for doctrine, for reproof, for correction, for instruction in righteousness, that the man of God may be complete, thoroughly equipped for every good work.*

We must be prudent or guarded when it comes to the influence our present climate of the world can have upon us. With the advent of social media, it has become increasingly easier to get caught up in ungodly chatter that can be mean and cruel to the extent of becoming bitter towards one another. The last thing we would want to do is to allow bitterness to take over to the extent that we end up backslidden to the degree we become defiled and

---

[50] Psalm 133:1-2
[51] Ephesians 4:1-3

no longer believe in the gospel of Jesus Christ. Yet, this is a possibility if we fail to obey our instructions in righteousness and not pursue peace with all people amid a crooked and perverse generation that's becoming more and more filled with hatred, violence, and bitterness. Therefore, we must make every effort to walk worthy of our calling with all lowliness, bearing with one another in love, endeavoring to keep the unity of the Spirit in the bond of peace.[52]

> We must be prudent or guarded when it comes to the influence our present climate of the world can have upon us. With the advent of social media, it has become so easy to get caught up in ungodly chatter that can be mean and cruel to the extent that we become bitter towards one another.

God gave us much instruction in His word on pursuing peace in all our relationships, especially with those who exhibit hostility. It starts with loving one another in the same manner God loves us. He gave His only begotten Son to be crucified by a cruel world towards Him. As Jesus hung on the cross, His words were, *"Father forgive them for they know not what they do."* Many in today's world are caught in the deceitful practices of the enemy of our faith, Satan. Many are caught up in the climate or the collective reasoning of our time. Those who have the loudest voices have little understanding of their deceit.

Our attitude should be the same as Jesus' when He said, *"Father forgive them for they don't know what they're doing."* We are to love our enemies just as Jesus did. Jesus also said we must be harmless as doves and wise serpents. We must allow the wisdom of God to filter the words that come out of our mouths.

Practically pursuing peace with those in opposition to us requires a reasonable degree of humility. With lowliness, we are to bear with one another in love. Through our humility and soft answers, their wrath is disarmed, allowing them to see the light of the gospel. When we are more concerned about winning others to the Lord through our godly examples, we are less concerned about winning arguments. Paul gives us some good advice on doing this in his second letter to His son in the faith, Timothy.

*2 **Timothy 2:23-26** But avoid foolish and ignorant disputes, knowing that they generate strife. [24] And a servant of the Lord must not quarrel but be gentle to all, able to teach, patient, [25] in humility correcting those who are in opposition, if God*

---

[52] Ephesians 4:1-3

perhaps will grant them repentance, so that they may know the truth, ²⁶ and that they may come to their senses and escape the snare of the devil, having been taken captive by him to do his will.

The more we understand that many in the world have lost their senses and have been taken captive by Satan, it helps to have compassion on them so that they, too, can escape the snares of the enemy through our gentle and peaceable approaches. So, let us pursue peace with all people.

May God bless you mightily as you endeavor to keep the unity of the Spirit in the bond of peace. May your love for one another shine brightly amid a crooked and perverse generation. May we be among those whom Jesus said, *"Blessed are the peacemakers, for they shall be called sons of God."*[53]

May the blessing of God's favor be upon you as you go forth in the might of His Spirit, transforming culture with the wisdom from above. Let us embrace one another in the Lord as Paul urges us to do in the following Scripture.

***Ephesians 4:1-3** I, therefore, the prisoner of the Lord, beseech you to walk worthy of the calling with which you were called, ² with all lowliness and gentleness, long-suffering, bearing with one another in love, ³ endeavoring to keep the unity of the Spirit in the bond of peace.*

Poem: Harmless as Doves

Caught in an environment filled with hate and violence, we ponder.
In the face of slanderers, despisers, haters, and more, we wander.
As pilgrims, we work out our salvation in this world, but not of it.
Pursuing peace with the self-absorbed, and haughty, we consider.
To love as Christ or get caught up in spirit of the culture we explore.

Like Jesus, wise as serpents, harmless as doves, we engage.
To be wise and speak, or harmless and quiet, we gage.
More concerned for the lost than the argument, we speak softly.
Going forth in Christ's love, giving ourselves to humility, we die.
Making every effort to be peaceable, refusing to quarrel, we vie.

Understanding the entrapments of Satan, we forgive behaviors.
With understanding and love, we speak in the presence of haters.
With hearts set on the power of His Spirit to transform, we speak.

---

[53] Matthew 5:9

The Rise of the Anointed Ones – Pursue Peace with All

In humility, correcting those in opposition, we speak with courage.
Pursuing peace in all relationships, we speak to encourage.

Prayer

Heavenly Father, help me be gentle and kind to those who oppose Your kingdom. Help me see past their present condition and how You desire to draw them into Your presence. Make me a peaceful person who is harmless as a dove but wise as a serpent.

~

Though some may ridicule you, may you be wise as a serpent but harmless as a dove as you respond well with kindness and gentleness.

Day 17

Trees of Righteousness

As Christians, God likens us to trees of righteousness, which speaks of how He views us despite our imperfections. By the blood of Jesus Christ, He perfected us forever. His righteousness has become ours. Knowing that He has perfected us forever gives us the confidence to stand before our Father in heaven, guilt free, no matter what we may have done.

Isaiah 61:3 *To console those who mourn in Zion, to give them beauty for ashes, the oil of joy for mourning, the garment of praise for the spirit of heaviness; that they may be called trees of righteousness, the planting of the LORD, that He may be glorified..*

In this passage of Scripture, we discover Christians referred to as trees of righteousness, the planting of the LORD. The Scriptures refer us to many things, all of which help to describe our relationship and purpose in Christ. Some of them are as follows: Saints, disciples, the Church, the bride of Christ, the army of God, sheep, the branch of the LORD, believers, Christians, the temple of the LORD, house of God, brothers and sisters, followers, living stones, the family of God and the elect.

The terms "Trees of Righteousness and the Planting of the LORD" have a lot to say about who we are in Christ and how He desires to relate to us. In John's gospel, Jesus speaks of the seed that must be planted in the earth for the trees of righteousness to come forth. These terms speak to the foundation of all that it means to be a follower of Christ.

John 12:23-24 *But Jesus answered them, saying, "The hour has come that the Son of Man should be glorified. ²⁴ Most assuredly, I say to you, unless a grain of wheat falls into the ground and dies, it remains alone; but if it dies, it produces much grain..*

The aforementioned passage is a powerful statement by Jesus. The essence of His message is He died to allow His sinless seed to be planted

The Rise of the Anointed Ones – Trees of Righteousness

in the earth so that He could produce a harvest of sons and daughters in His likeness, which He would fill with His righteousness. As the Scripture says, *"For He made Him who knew no sin to be sin for us, that we might become the righteousness of God in Him."*[54] Because we are the planting of the LORD, we're called trees of righteousness. When Jesus went to the cross, He perfected forever those who are being sanctified.[55] In the Father's eyes, we are just as sinless as Jesus. He became sin for us so that He can now call us trees of righteousness as we stand in His righteousness rather than our own..

We have been planted as our Heavenly Father's trees of righteousness to bring forth the knowledge of His kingdom, His holiness, and the transforming power of the Holy Spirit to a lost and dying world. As the Father sent Jesus into the world, so have we been sent. We are the result, or the harvest of His seed that was buried in the earth through His death, burial, and resurrection.

Isaiah 61:11 *For as the earth brings forth its bud, as the garden causes the things that are sown in it to spring forth, so the Lord GOD will cause righteousness and praise to spring forth before all the nations.*

Our world is spinning out of control, with people all around us giving into fear and losing hope. For those deeply rooted in their identity as children of God, who are perfected forever by the blood of Christ through the transforming power of the Holy Spirit, He destines to flourish. They will never cease bearing fruit, even when seasons of deep darkness cover the land. Therefore, God has destined His anointed ones to rise and thrive in the house of the Lord. He has planted us to bring forth His glory for such a time as this..

Psalms 92:12-15 *The righteous shall flourish like a palm tree, he shall grow like a cedar in Lebanon.* [13] *Those who are planted in the house of the LORD shall flourish in the courts of our God.* [14] *They shall still bear fruit in old age; they shall be fresh and flourishing,* [15] *to declare that the LORD is upright; He is my rock, and there is no unrighteousness in Him..*

If we are to fulfill all that God's word says about who we are in Christ, our roots must go deep into who we are in Him. God has called us to let our lights shine brightly to a lost and troubled world. If our roots are shallow, we will never experience His fullness that fills all and all with His glory.[56]

---

[54] 2 Corinthians 5:21
[55] Hebrews 10:1
[56] Ephesians 1:23

The Rise of the Anointed Ones – Trees of Righteousness

To be a part of all that God is doing, we must allow our hearts to go deep into the soil we've been planted for this prophetic purpose to come to pass in our individual lives.

***Jeremiah 17:7-8** Blessed is the man who trusts in the LORD, and whose hope is the LORD. ⁸ For he shall be like a tree planted by the waters, which spreads out its roots by the river, and will not fear when heat comes; but its leaf will be green and will not be anxious in the year of drought, nor will cease from yielding fruit.*

> Our world is spinning out of control, with people all around us giving into fear and losing hope. For those deeply rooted in their identity as children of God, who are perfected forever by the blood of Christ through the transforming power of the Holy Spirit, He destines to flourish.

As we embrace the perfect righteousness we have in Christ, the same fullness Jesus walked in while He was on the earth belongs to us. We are His body that came forth from His sinless seed buried in the ground. As sons and daughters, the Holy Spirit anoints us to rise in the fullness of the stature of Christ with His glory filling the earth.[57] As trees of righteousness, our roots will continually be watered from the river that flows from His throne, enabling us to go forth in His fullness.

Poem: Trees of Righteousness

Coming in the likeness of man, without sin, He gave of Himself.
Planted in the earth as a tree of righteousness, He gives birth.
Coming forth in His likeness, trees of righteousness appear.
With one offering, made perfect in His righteousness, we proclaim.
Called trees of righteousness, we glorify Him, who gave of Himself.

With roots going deep into Him, who became sin, we follow.
Immersed in His identity, we die daily, embracing His cross.
Allowing His likeness to come forth from glory to glory, we rejoice.
Like a palm tree, in His presence, we bear fruit and flourish.
Called trees of righteousness, we proclaim Him who gave all.

Roots spread with trust and hope in Him; He refreshes the soul.
Roots going deep into the soil planted, fruitfulness appears.
Watered from the river of life, there's no need for anxiety in drought.

---

[57] Ephesians 1:22-23

The Rise of the Anointed Ones – Trees of Righteousness

Called to spread righteousness to the nations, we shine brightly.
Called trees of righteousness, we go forth in His transforming power.

In His righteousness, we go forth in His fullness, fulfilling His Word.
With the prophetic word to fill all with His presence, His power spreads.
With signs and wonders, His trees of righteousness proclaim His majesty.
Responding heartedly, multitudes in the valley of decision, He draws.
Called trees of righteousness, to Him who draws, we give applause.

Prayer

Heavenly Father, help me to fully understand all that You accomplished for me on the cross. I desire to be a tree of righteousness whose roots go deep into the soil in which I have been planted. Help me to be all that you have destined me to be.

~

May the Lord bless you mightily as a tree of righteousness as you go forth in the fullness of the stature of Christ fulfilling His word to a lost generation.

Day 18

Flourish Where You're Planted

As born-again Christians, we are the planting of the Lord. We are the precious plants in whom the Father delights. He is the Gardener who delights in the seeds He planted. Our Heavenly Father assures us that He will faithfully attend His garden. His desire is that we would all flourish where He has planted us as He faithfully tends to each plant.

Psalms 92:12-15 *The righteous shall flourish like a palm tree, he shall grow like a cedar in Lebanon.* [13] *Those who are planted in the house of the LORD shall flourish in the courts of our God.* [14] *They shall still bear fruit in old age; they shall be fresh and flourishing,* [15] *to declare that the LORD is upright; He is my rock, and there is no unrighteousness in Him..*

As we enter our current seasons of nourishment, it will be vital to discern our placement or field of ministry in the Lord's harvest. Many revival waves will come and go before the culmination of all that the prophets have prophesied.[58] Therefore, we need to be busily involved in our places of ministry. The Father's desire is for each of us to flourish in the place He has set us. With the Church on the verge of one of the greatest revivals known to humanity, the need to know our placement is expedient.

I Corinthians 12:18 *But now God has set the members, each one of them, in the body just as He pleased..*

It is helpful to understand God fashioned and formed us in our mother's womb. He saw our substance when we were still unformed and secretly made. In His book, He has already written our days.[59] He has now set us

---

[58] Ephesians 1:22-23
[59] Psalm 139:13-16

in places conducive to His divine design. God has strategically placed all of us to function in perfect harmony with His purposes. As the wind of His Spirit blows on the dry bones spoken by Ezekiel, the prophet, we are destined to rise as His anointed ones in His glory,[60] in the place He planted and called us to function. We should ask ourselves, "Do I know the area or calling God has specifically designed for me, or am I still groping about trying to figure it out?

> The Father's desire is for each of us to flourish in the place He has set us. With the Church on the verge of one of the greatest revivals known to humanity, the need to know our placement is expedient.

I Corinthians 7:2 Brethren, let each one remain with God in that state in which he was called.

To know our place is to look around and see where we are presently planted. Your life is where God desires you to grow. Your life is your harvest field, the place where God commissioned you to flourish. Your field is where you are to develop the fruit of the Spirit and express the gifts, both the innate and the supernatural in the Spirit. Therefore, it is expedient for us to put on the new man or the character of Christ so that we are perfectly positioned, when the wind of the Spirit blows upon us.

John 3:8 *The wind blows where it wishes, and you hear the sound of it but cannot tell where it comes from and where it goes. So is everyone who is born of the Spirit.*

Because we don't know when or where the wind blows from, we must be ready in all situations in the places God strategically planted us. Otherwise, we miss the opportunities the Lord of the harvest brings our way. When we are in position with an expectation to be used, we experience divine appointments..

John 4:35 *Do you not say, 'There are still four months and then comes the harvest'? Behold, I say to you, lift your eyes and look at the fields, for they are already white for harvest!*

If our testimony is compromised, the wind of the Spirit will have little effect on those we come in contact within our harvest fields. Therefore, Paul told Timothy to be an excellent example to unbelievers and believers. His words to Timothy are vitally important to all of us if we flourish in the places God has planted us. As we prepare ourselves to be used mightily in

---

[60] Ezekiel 34:4-10

the Lord's Harvest by developing what Paul encourages Timothy to do in the passage below, we not only save ourselves but those in our wake.

I Timothy 4:12-16 Let no one despise your youth, but be an example to the believers in word, in conduct, in love, in spirit, in faith, in purity. [13] Till I come, give attention to reading, to exhortation, to doctrine. [14] Do not neglect the gift that is in you, which was given to you by prophecy with the laying on of the hands of the eldership. [15] Meditate on these things; give yourself entirely to them, that your progress may be evident to all. [16] Take heed to yourself and to the doctrine. Continue in them, for in doing this, you will save both yourself and those who hear you..

Poem: Bloom Where You're Planted

As the breath of God touches, new life springs forth.
Intimately made in secret, our days He fashions.
Called according to His purposes, He continually forms.
Knowing our beginning and endings, He plants.
Planted in the house of the Lord, He causes to flourish.

Submitting to His plans and purposes, we discern.
Looking up, His field of harvest, we recognize.
Embracing gifts and talents, we discern our places.
Whatever our hands find to do, we do mightily.
Knowing He has set us accordingly, we labor.

With testimonies intact, we sow faithfully in our fields.
As others stand by, we give ourselves wholeheartedly.
In conduct, love, faith, and purity, we seek not to offend.
Planted in His field, we flourish in all that we touch.
With the harvest ripe, we labor and flourish in His courts.

In the valley of decision, multitudes wait to be chosen.
With a great harvest in sight, more laborers are planted and sent.
Filling, all in all, His glory settles upon those who flourish.
As His glory reconciles, multitudes convert and spring forth.
As the breath of God touches, we stand together in unity.

Prayer

Lord, I offer you my life as a worker in Your harvest fields. May I take the placement seriously You set me in. Help me to be faithful in all that You have given to me. Help me to be sensitive to those you have placed in my path. Help me to be a testimony of Your grace and righteousness as I go forth into your harvest fields.

The Rise of the Anointed Ones – Flourish Where You're Planted

~

May God bless you richly as you flourish in the place, He planted you. Then, as His glory settles, may you become all that He envisioned for you.

Day 19

The Word Mixed with Faith

Jesus said, if we have faith, nothing is impossible. What must we do to inherit this kind of faith? What is the key? Throughout God's Word, we have many wonderful promises that not only guarantee us an abundant life but also assure us of a life filled with purpose and vision. All the promises of God are yes and amen, but it takes faith on our part to have His words transformed into a life-giving faith that produces the realized benefit of the promises. The key to unlocking our faith is found in the following Scripture.

Hebrews 4:2 For indeed the gospel was preached to us as well as to them; but the word which they heard did not profit them, not being mixed with faith in those who heard it.

From the above Scripture, we see that the key to receiving all that God has for us through our relationship with Jesus Christ is mixing His word with faith. The question then becomes, how do we mix God's word with faith? There are three essential elements involved for this to happen.

The first element is to have ears to hear. How many times did Jesus say, *"To him who has ears to hear?"* He said it many times throughout His ministry while here on earth. We must have ears to hear if the seed of God's word is to fall on the good ground of our hearts.

Luke 8:8 But others fell on good ground, sprang up, and yielded a crop a hundredfold. When He had said these things, He cried, "He who has ears to hear, let him hear!"

To hear in such a way that produces faith, we must first open our hearts to God's word in humility and brokenness. The Pharisees and the Sadducees couldn't hear the words of Jesus because of the hardness of their hearts. Their hearts were not sufficiently plowed to have Jesus' words produce faith in their lives. They didn't approach Jesus with broken and contrite hearts, which would have entailed them coming humbly before God

The Rise of the Anointed Ones – Mixing the Word with Faith

acknowledging their sin while proclaiming His goodness. The Pharisees and the Sadducees were stuck in their righteousness, which blinded them to the truth of God's word that produces faith. They didn't have ears to hear. Do we have ears to hear, or are we also stuck in our righteousness? As we purpose to allow God to break up the fallow ground of our hearts, we should respond to God's word in such a way that the seeds of faith and truth get planted in our hearts.

The second element is coming into agreement with God's word. For the Word and faith to mix properly involves coming into an agreement with God's word once we hear it. In writing to the Romans, Paul said, *"So then faith comes by hearing, and hearing by the word of God."*[61] Once God plants the seed of truth, it must be adequately watered and nurtured for it to come to fruition. Because all Scripture comes from the inspiration of God and is profitable for doctrine and instruction in righteousness, we must purpose in our hearts to come into agreement with it.[62]

> All the promises of God are yes and amen, but it takes faith on our part to have His words transformed into a life-giving faith that produces the realized benefit of the promises.

The nurturing process begins as we believe God's word with our hearts, even if we don't understand it. Then, as we believe whatever God says about us and what He has given, we begin to confess what we believe. As the apostle, Paul said, *"And since we have the same spirit of faith, according to what is written, 'I believed, and therefore I spoke,' we also believe and therefore speak."*[63] Our confession becomes our first act of believing in what He has said. We then move from faith to faith by confessing our beliefs as He reveals His righteousness in greater degrees. Moving from faith to faith by acknowledging what we believe leads us to the third element of mixing His word with faith.

The third element is our obedience, requiring action. Faith without works is dead.[64] The Israelites were given many wonderful promises following their deliverance from their Egyptian bondage. For them to receive all the wonderful promises God had given them, they had to act on their faith. As they acted on their faith through obedience, it became a continuing process as they came into the fulfillment of all that God had

---

[61] Romans 10:17
[62] 2 Timothy 3:16
[63] 2 Corinthians 4:13
[64] James 2:14-18

promised them. The same is true for us as we go from faith to faith. Our growth and maturity in Christ are a series of hearing, believing, and acting.

Isaiah 1:18-19 "*Come now, and let us reason together,*" *Says the LORD, "Though your sins are like scarlet, they shall be as white as snow; though they are red like crimson, they shall be as wool. If you are willing and obedient, You shall eat the good of the land." If you are willing and obedient, You shall eat the good of the land."*

I John 3:22 And whatever we ask, we receive from Him because we keep His commandments and do those things that are pleasing in His sight.

May God bless you richly as you have ears to hear all that the Father desires to pour into your spirit through Jesus Christ. May you come into agreement with everything He has spoken to you through His word as you act upon your faith to receive the promises. May you profit from all that God's Holy Word has for you as you mix His word with your faith..

Poem: Pressing on in Faith,

With contrite hearts, we stand with ears to hear.
In promises given, we stand ready to possess.
As faith comes by hearing, our hearts draw near.
Breaking up the fallow ground, the seed, He imparts.
With the seed planted, roots go deep into our hearts.

Unbelief departing, in the power of His Word, we believe.
As the word of faith comes forth, we stand in agreement.
Faith reaching to apprehend, we lay hold, pressing forward.
Believing in the inspiration of Scripture, we receive.
With all things about life promised, we conceive.

Knowing God oversees all, we respond accordingly.
Knowing He never leaves nor forsakes, we press continually.
Going from faith to faith, obedience carries us forward.
Giving according to needs, He loads with benefits expressed.
Surprising us at how well He cares, we're blessed.

Blessed beyond measure, we enjoy all springing forth.
Pressed down, shaken together, and running over, He blesses.
Faith imparting, His generosity continually reveals His treasures.
Knowing our needs before asking, He rewards faithfulness.
Living by faith, His righteousness, we experience in all things.

Prayer

As the disciples prayed, *"Lord increase our faith,"* I pray, Lord, increase my faith. Help me to hear when You speak to my heart. Help me boldly confess and act upon all that You direct me to do.

~

May your heart and soul be filled with excitement and adventure as you press forward, mixing God's word with faith as He speaks into your spirit.

Day 20

Becoming a Pattern of Good Works

Even though we are saved by grace and not by works, we have been created in Christ Jesus for good works. We are His workmanship, which means our goals should encompass a pattern of good works as Paul encourages us to do.

Titus 2:6-8 *Likewise, exhort the young men to be sober-minded, in all things showing yourself to be a pattern of good works; ⁷ in doctrine showing integrity, reverence, incorruptibility, ⁸ sound speech that cannot be condemned, that one who is an opponent may be ashamed, having nothing evil to say of you.*

To be a person who exhibits a pattern of good works involves making sure works are a significant part of our rhythm in life as we follow Christ. The grace of God in us is partially for the purpose of producing good works in Christ. You might say, grace produces His workmanship in us. Jesus, Himself went about doing good works, and we are to emulate Him in all things. His life was a pattern of good works.

Ephesians 2:8-10 *For by grace you have been saved through faith, and that not of yourselves; it is the gift of God, ⁹ not of works, lest anyone should boast. ¹⁰ For we are His workmanship, created in Christ Jesus for good works, which God prepared beforehand that we should walk in them.*

Titus 2:13-14 *looking for the blessed hope and glorious appearing of our great God and Savior Jesus Christ, ¹⁴ who gave Himself for us, that He might redeem us from every lawless deed and purify for Himself His own special people, zealous for good works..*

In today's Christianity, there seems to be more emphasis on exploring our liberties in Christ rather than disciplining ourselves to walk in integrity, reverence, incorruptibility, and sound speech that cannot be condemned. In Paul's letter to Timothy, he was encouraged to be an example in all

The Rise of the Anointed Ones – Becoming a Pattern of Good Works

things. *He said, "Let no one despise your youth, but be an example to the believers in word, in conduct, in love, in spirit, in faith, in purity."*[65]

Are we so busy playing spiritual games with God that we miss the mark of what our true calling in God is? God called us to be zealous for good works because we are Christ's workmanship. We are the vessels He is now using to transform the lives of those we meet by showing ourselves a pattern of good works. We have the grace of God working mightily in us to perform all kinds of good works just like Jesus did. Paul's testimony was, *"To this end I also labor, striving according to His working which works in me mightily."* [66]

As believers in Christ, we have the same Holy Spirit working in us that performed mightily in Christ and the apostle Paul. In writing to the church at Ephesus, Paul wrote, *"And what is the exceeding greatness of His power toward us who believe, according to the working of His mighty power which He worked in Christ when He raised Him from the dead and seated Him at His right hand in the heavenly places."*[67] Let us rise as the anointed ones in a belief that lays hold of the power working in us while making ourselves a pattern of good works.

Just as Jesus went about doing good and healing all who the devil oppressed, the body of Christ must be about our Father's business as Jesus was. Therefore, our Father in heaven has commissioned us to go into our harvest fields as a pattern of good works so that those oppressed by the world and Satan's influence can be healed and experience the same saving grace we've experienced.

> To be a person who exhibits a pattern of good works involves making sure works are a significant part of our rhythm in life. The grace of God in us is partially for the purpose of producing good works in us as we follow Christ.

Will you rise to the call of God and give yourself to this generation, or will you sit by while our cultures lie in ruin and become bound in the darkness that is spreading rapidly through the world? Now is the time to respond by laboring and striving according to the working of the Holy Spirit, who is ready to catapult us forward in the grace of God. Let us be obedient to all

---

[65] 1 Timothy 4:12
[66] Colossians 1:29
[67] Ephesians 1:19-20

The Rise of the Anointed Ones – Becoming a Pattern of Good Works

that the Lord Jesus Christ calls us to do in the harvest field He has chosen us to labor in.

I Corinthians 15:58 Therefore, my beloved brethren, be steadfast, immovable, always abounding in the work of the Lord, knowing that your labor is not in vain in the Lord.

Poem: Becoming Christ's Workmanship

By grace, as His workmanship, we freely give sufficiently.
Sober minded in all that we do, we present ourselves freely.
As vessels of honor, we cling to Him as our righteousness.
Setting us free from bondages, we serve without reticence.
Giving ourselves freely, we stand zealous without arrogance.

Exhibiting a pattern of good works, we cling to His sufficiency.
Knowing that He's perfect in all, we trust in His proficiency.
Experiencing grace in all we do; we maintain good works.
In reverence to His creative abilities, we give ourselves freely.
As life's rhythms establish, good works multiply abundantly.

Giving ourselves to His Spirit, His creative power works mightily.
Working fervently in us, as His workmanship, we strive accordingly.
Performing mightily in and through, He reveals new divine abilities.
With divine abilities secured, purpose and vision expand widely.
Knowing the exceeding greatness of His power, we submit willingly.

As vision and purpose expand, new adventures await us.
Unlimited as His workmanship, we experience new-found treasures.
As freedom and liberty express, zeal for good works takes over.
Filled with zeal from above, given to His workmanship, we vow.
Giving praise and glory to Him who works magnificently, we bow.

Prayer

Father God, help me to be mindful of all that the Holy Spirit is working in my life so that I will be a pattern of good works You have ordained for me. Help me be faithful to use the spiritual gifts You have sown into my life. I give myself to You as Your workmanship that I may glorify You in all that I do.

~

May God bless you richly as you put on the garments of Christ, making no provision for the flesh, and becoming a pattern of good works.

Day 21

Spiritually Inflamed With Spiritual Gifts

One of the great blessings of becoming a born-again Christian is receiving spiritual gifts from the Father above. It's one thing to receive a gift, but it's another thing to learn how to use it to the extent that it becomes a mighty force in your arsenal of spiritual weapons. The Father desires to set our hearts on fire as He gives birth to the spiritual gifts within. To adequately bring the gift forth God has given will involve stirring it up from a tiny ember into a roaring fire. As one of His anointed ones, it will cause you to embrace the Lord's harvest as one of His flames of fire.

2 Timothy 1:6-7 Therefore, I remind you to stir up the gift of God which is in you through the laying on of my hands. For God has not given us a spirit of fear but of power and of love and of a sound mind. ⁷ For God has not given us a spirit of fear but of power and of love and of a sound mind..

If we are to mature into what God commissioned us to be and do in Christ, we must understand how our gifts and purpose work in relationship to His goals.[68] Knowing that the Father called us to come into the fullness of the stature of Christ, spiritual gifts are a necessity.[69] They become a part of our identity in Christ and are essential for use in the ministries God called forth in our lives. He freely gave them, but it takes total immersion into the Holy Spirit by pressing into His gifts by asking, seeking, and knocking for them to be released. As the apostle Paul so aptly said, *"I press on, that I may lay hold of that which Christ Jesus has also laid hold of me."* If we are to lay hold of all that's been freely given to us, we must do the same. We begin by asking, seeking, and knocking.

---

[68] 2 Timothy 1:9
[69] Ephesians 4:12-13

The Rise of the Anointed Ones –Inflamed with Spiritual Gifts

***Luke 11:9-10,13** So I say to you, ask, and it will be given to you; seek, and you will find; knock, and it will be opened to you. ¹⁰ For everyone who asks receives, and he who seeks finds, and to him who knocks it will be opened. ¹³ If you then, being evil, know how to give good gifts to your children, how much more will your heavenly Father give the Holy Spirit to those who ask Him..*

As we approach the end-time environment and all that God desires to do before the second coming of Christ, it will be imperative to recognize how important it is for each of us to discover our spiritual gifts. In his letter to the Corinthian church, Paul clarifies why spiritual gifts are necessary for every believer to develop. Notice how he lumps gifts, ministries, and activities together. They all work together for the evidence of the manifestation of the Spirit..

***I Corinthians 12:4-7** There are diversities of gifts, but the same Spirit. ⁵ There are differences of ministries, but the same Lord. ⁶ And there are diversities of activities, but it is the same God who works all in all. ⁷ But the manifestation of the Spirit is given to each one for the profit of all..*

> If we are to mature into what God commissioned us to be and do in Christ, we must understand how our gifts and purpose work in relationship to His goals. Knowing that the Father called us to come into the fullness of the stature of Christ, spiritual gifts are a necessity.

In the above passage, the word "works" means active operation, productive, powerful, dynamic, efficient, fervent, and mighty in showing forth. The term *"manifestation"* means to make visible, clear, and known. With these two definitions in mind, we can see it's God's desire for us to be vigorous and mighty in showing forth and making His power visible through the gifts of the Spirit. As members of His body, we are to be zealous, active, productive, efficient, and mighty in manifesting the gifts of the Spirit for the benefit of the body as a whole. When this happens, we become the flames of fire He has destined us to be.[70]

The gifts of the Spirit are an integral part of our spiritual growth and function within the body of Christ. Paul said concerning spiritual gifts, *"I don't want you to be ignorant nor come short in any gift while eagerly waiting for the second coming of Christ."* [71] We must understand that a significant part of God's will and purpose is for us to discover what our

---

[70] Psalm 104:3-4
[71] 1 Corinthians 1:7, 12:1

gift or gifts are. Without them, our efforts in ministry will be motivated out of self-sufficiency rather than relying on God's sufficiency.

When Paul mentions to Timothy to stir up the gift given to him, the word *"stir"* implies seeking, asking, and knocking until the manifestation of the gift is made clear. In the same way, that fire bursts forth from blowing on an ember or spark until it explodes into a flame is what we must do to experience the manifestation of spiritual gifts.

As we are faithful to develop a relationship with the Holy Spirit by pressing into all that He has for us, He is faithful to search the Father's heart for what He desires to pour into our lives. The Father knows the perfect gift that fits how He has designed and created us and is therefore delighted when we begin to ask, seek, and knock.

1 Corinthians 2:10-12 But God has revealed them to us through His Spirit. For the Spirit searches all things, yes, the deep things of God. [11] For what man knows the things of a man except the spirit of the man which is in him? Even so, no one knows the things of God except the Spirit of God. [12] Now we have received, not the spirit of the world, but the Spirit who is from God, that we might know the things that have been freely given to us by God.

It is crucial for us to understand there is no magic formula for discovering and utilizing your spiritual gift other than developing a genuine relationship with the Holy Spirit. Once you discover your gift, you must continually inflame it by looking for opportunities to use it. As Paul wrote to the Romans, *"Having then gifts differing according to our grace that is given to us, let us use them."*

To use the gifts freely given to us, we must find opportunities to practice them. Practice, practice, practice until they become a flaming fire. Therefore, stir your gift until the ember or spark bursts into a flame of fire that continually ministers to others. As you do, you become the gift of God to others as you faithfully minister with the anointing you have freely received.

1 Peter 4:10 As each one has received a gift, minister it to one another as good stewards of the manifold grace of God.

Poem: Hearts Aflame

From the Holy Spirit, we seek to discover.
To achieve, we ask and knock to uncover.
Destined to be flames of fire, we breathe.

The Rise of the Anointed Ones –Inflamed with Spiritual Gifts

Blowing on the embers, sparks ignite.
As the heart inflames, in Him, we delight.

Given to His will, we go forth in His sufficiency.
In His proficiency, faith explodes into flames.
As faith activates, ministry opportunities appear.
Engulfed in flames, hearts turn to God for more.
Delighted in His manifested presence, we hear.

Filled with inflamed passion, sparks ignite many.
Caught up, in the moment, others are reaped in plenty.
No longer feeding on useless things, we freely partake.
As fervency drives, His Spirit fills vessels abundantly.
Given to the wind of His Spirit, gifts flow freely.

Fully developed, flames of fire, we will be.
Harvest fields, we go, igniting fires everywhere.
With gifts released, hearts everywhere catch fire.
With harvest fields white for harvest, laborers multiply.
Giving glory to God for gifts given, we stand humbled.

Prayer

Heavenly Father, I come to you today asking, seeking, and knocking for You to fill me with the fullness of Your Spirit. Allow Your gifts to come forth that I might freely minister to others out of Your abundance that freely flows out of my life.

~

May your heart be inflamed with the anointing of the Holy Spirit as He pours His gifts into your life.

Day 22

Finding Refuge In the Secret Place

As Bob Dylan wrote many years ago during a season of cultural upheaval and change, *"The Times, They Are a Changing,"* so it is today. Our world today is rapidly changing right before our eyes, with political unrest, violence, wickedness, and disorder as seemingly insurmountable problems and troubles confront us daily. However, amid all that is happening in our world today, our God is a stronghold and place of refuge. We have a secret place to dwell amid all that is taking place.

Psalm 37:39-40 *(NIV) The salvation of the righteous comes from the Lord; He is their stronghold in time of trouble. ⁴⁰ The Lord helps them and delivers them; he delivers them from the wicked and saves them because they take refuge in him.*

As significant upheaval and change occur at alarming rates, we must put our faith in God and His ability to protect and keep us secure. With a worldwide pandemic, cancel culture, racial riots, the polarization of political systems, mass murders, and more, we find ourselves facing turmoil, fear, depression, and anxiety as crime, violence, and death increase in a hate-filled world gone wrong. Troublous and difficult times are upon us and will most likely continue until Jesus returns. Therefore, we must put our hope in God and His place of refuge. We must find that secret place that keeps us secure in Him.

The challenge for all of us is to find refuge in God, not only during difficult times but continually. It could be that God is allowing what's taking place in our world today so that we learn to take refuge in His secret place before things get out of control to a greater degree than what's happening now. God has a secret place for us to discover as He works His will and desires in us.

The Rise of the Anointed Ones – Finding Refuge in the Secret Place

As the aforementioned Scripture implies, God desires to be a stronghold for us during difficult and trying times. Before He can be a stronghold, we must first learn what it means to take refuge in Him. He says, He delivers, saves, and helps us because we take refuge in Him. We must ask ourselves what it means to take refuge in God and what that looks like? To begin with, let's start with a good definition of the word "refuge." It is a condition of being safe or sheltered from pursuit, danger, or trouble. We know that troublous and perilous times will be a permanent part of the end time environment, so as Christians, we desperately need to discover and hide in the place of refuge the psalmist speaks of, which means making the Most High our place of refuge.

The book of Nahum speaks of this place of refuge when the prophet says, *"The Lord is good, a stronghold in the day of trouble; and He knows those who trust in Him."*[72] Nahum provides us with the key to opening the door to the place of refuge God has for us. He says God knows those who trust in Him. Trust is the key because we will lack the faith to step into something unknown or unfamiliar. Without trust, we will continue to walk

> The challenge for all of us is to find our refuge in God, not only during difficult times but continually. It could be that God is allowing what's taking place in our world today so that we learn to take refuge in Him before things get out of control to a greater degree than what's happening now.

in our understanding rather than leaning on God's ways and wisdom. We must learn to acknowledge God in all of our ways, aligning ourselves with the commands and principles found in His Word. He is our peace and security amid all that's happening in our world today, which is different from what the world has to offer, as John reminds us from the words of Jesus.

John 14:27 *Peace I leave with you, My peace I give to you; not as the world gives do I give to you. Let not your heart be troubled, neither let it be afraid.*

John 16:33 *These things I have spoken to you, that in Me you may have peace. In the world, you will have tribulation, but be of good cheer, I have overcome the world.*

As we can see, these two passages of Scripture and others speak of how we find our refuge in clinging to Jesus. When we allow the Holy Spirit to guide us, He takes us to this beautiful place of refuge. He gives us peace amid the storms by declaring all that's in the heart of the Father concerning

---

[72] Nahum 1:7

The Rise of the Anointed Ones – Finding Refuge in the Secret Place

whatever adversity we may be facing.[73] As we give ourselves to the Holy Spirit's work wholeheartedly, we fully embrace Jesus as the Lord of our lives, which releases the Father's heart and desires toward us.

By putting our faith and trust in the Most High, we adjust quickly to difficult situations that come our way during turbulent times. We discover the peace of God and His security no matter what our circumstances may be. By believing and trusting in the Father to speak to us through the Word and Spirit, we won't get swept away with the herd mentality that's invading our world today. Instead, we find ourselves resting in a place of safety and shelter that's free from the fear, depression, and anxiety that's raging across the landscapes of our world. Though our times are rapidly changing, we can find refuge in the arms of our Lord and Savior, Jesus Christ, as we abide under the shadow of the Almighty just as He promised.

Psalm 91:1-2 *He who dwells in the **secret place** of the Most High shall abide under the shadow of the Almighty. ² I will say of the Lord, He is my refuge and my fortress; My God, **in Him I will trust.***

Psalm 91:9-11 *Because you have made the Lord, who is my refuge, even the Most High, your dwelling place, ¹⁰ no evil shall befall you, nor shall any plague come near your dwelling; ¹¹ for He shall give His angels charge over you, to keep you in all your ways.*

May God bless you richly as you make the Lord your refuge and dwelling place. May His angels continually watch over you. May you discover the secret place the Lord has fashioned just for you, where you can hide amid adversity.

Poem: Finding Refuge in God

Caught in a torrential downpour of hate and violence, we scream.
Fear and turmoil prevailing, birthing anxiety, we no longer dream.
Lost in a world of changing values, crime and violence take over.
Bewildered and confused during difficult times, we look for cover.
Suffering loss from stolen dreams, our souls cry out for refuge.

Looking to the heavens above, in desperation, we cry for release.
Cautiously, reaching for a ray of hope, we look to You for peace.
Looking for a stronghold to latch onto, Your righteousness extends.
Drowning in a sea of sorrows, we reach for Your hand in weariness.
Quickly grabbing hold, Your righteousness extends in forgiveness.

---

[73] John 16:33

The Rise of the Anointed Ones – Finding Refuge in the Secret Place

In a moment, the warmth of Your goodness fills as hope abounds.
No longer drowning in sorrow, You place us on solid ground.
As storms continue to rage around the world, You speak of trust.
As righteousness takes hold, a stronghold You give for security.
Speaking softly, You reveal the secret place to dwell in surety.

As fear and depression dissipate, Your peace floods amid storms.
Clinging to the stronghold of love, Your righteousness transforms.
Declaring the Father's heart, Your Spirit guides through adversity.
Hiding in Your shadow, peace fills our hearts with exuberance.
Following the Father's way, we dwell safely in assurance.

Aligned with His commands and principles, trust conforms.
Discovery of His secret place, refuge is found amid the storms.
Under the shadow of Your wings, angels stand guard.
Though storms rage, in our secret place, we dwell untroubled.
Though the times change rapidly, in His love, we're shielded.

Prayer

Heavenly Father, thank you for providing a secret place to dwell amid the storms that are raging across the world's landscapes. Give me wisdom and understanding to lean upon You as You hide me in the shadow of Your wings. Lead me to the secret place You have fashioned for the person You have created me to be.

~

As you make the Lord your refuge, may you be filled with His peace and comfort in all that you do.

Day 23

Clothed in Humility

Humility is the primary character trait that allows Christ to conform us into His image. Without humility, we don't have a starting point. If we are to be vessels of honor who go into the Lord's harvest fields as His anointed ones, with His sufficiency working in and through us to see others transformed, humility before God and others is a must.

Colossians 3:12 *Therefore, as the elect of God, holy and beloved, put on tender mercies, kindness, humility, meekness, long suffering.*

When you look at the beatitudes that Jesus shared with His early followers, you see humility as the bottom rung of the ladder of all that He shared. Jesus said, *"Blessed are the poor in spirit, for theirs is the kingdom of heaven."* At another time when His disciples were arguing about who was the greatest, He placed a little child in front of them and said, *"Assuredly, I say to you, unless you are converted and become as little children, you will by no means enter the kingdom of heaven."* Notice, He begins with the word "Assuredly." In other words, there are no shortcuts.

Being clothed in humility is the beginning of our journey in Christ. In every aspect of our lives, we must become like-minded in Him, especially in humility, if we are to enjoy the blessings, He desires to daily impart into our spirits. Paul's letter to the Philippian church expresses this thought perfectly.

Philippians 2:5-8 *Let this mind be in you, which was also in Christ Jesus, ⁶ who, being in the form of God, did not consider it robbery to be equal with God, ⁷ but made Himself of no reputation, taking the form of a bondservant, and coming in the likeness of men. ⁸ And being found in appearance as a man, He humbled Himself and became obedient to the point of death, even the death of the cross.*

The Rise of the Anointed Ones – Clothed in Humility

Just as Christ had to humble Himself, so must we. Suppose we haven't come to the place where we have humbled ourselves before God or have been humbled by Him. In that case, pride will manifest itself in a myriad ways in our service areas to the body of Christ and our relationships with one another. As Christians, humility is an essential way of life for us, just as it was for Jesus.

Andrew Murray once said, *"Humility before God is nothing if not proved in humility before men."*

Therefore, we must clothe ourselves in humility. Otherwise, we are nothing more than wild tares in the kingdom with our works burned, yet being saved so as by fire, whatever that means.

1 Corinthians 3:11-15 For no other foundation can anyone lay than that which is laid, which is Jesus Christ. ¹² Now if anyone builds on this foundation with gold, silver, precious stones, wood, hay, straw, ¹³ each one's work will become clear; for the Day will declare it, because it will be revealed by fire; and the fire will test each one's work, of what sort it is. ¹⁴ If anyone's work which he has built on it endures, he will receive a reward. ¹⁵ If anyone's work is burned, he will suffer loss; but he himself will be saved, yet so as through fire.

> Being clothed in humility is the beginning of our journey in Christ. In every aspect of our lives, we must become like-minded in Him, especially in humility, if we are to enjoy the daily blessings, He desires to impart into our spirits.

Let's keep in mind that Jesus is building His Church out of our lives. It will be a Church that will not only stand against all of Satan's wiles and authority but will be a shining example and replica of the life of Jesus while on earth. As we allow humility and all the attitudes in Christ to possess our lives, Jesus adequately fits and frames us together as living stones. growing into a holy temple as a dwelling place for God in the Spirit. Jesus is building His Church out of the living stones that consist of who we are as we faithfully humble ourselves in His presence. Jesus will have a Church that contains the glory that fills the earth with His presence as the following scripture reveals His prophetic purpose.

Ephesians 1:22-23 And He put all things under His feet and gave Him to be head over all things to the Church, ²³ which is His body, the fullness of Him who fills all in all.

In the above passage, Paul reveals how the Church Jesus is building will look when His fullness that fills all in all becomes reality. The same fullness that was evident in the life of Jesus during His time of ministry on earth will be evidenced in His body, the Church. However, this evidence will only happen as we humble ourselves before God and the people, He chooses to place us next to as lively stones. Therefore, we have a responsibility to humble ourselves so that He can exalt us in due time.

Poem: Glorifying God with our Lives

With trust as our guide, we give all glory to God.
With desire to succeed, we come to trust in Him.
Knowing He knows all things, free reign, we give Him.
Content, whether abasing or abounding, we trust.
Setting our hearts according to His word, we adjust.

Knowing His thoughts are higher than ours, we thrive.
To Him who knows past, present, and future, we derive.
Not given to our perceptions, to Him, glory is given.
Desiring to succeed, we no longer scheme to manipulate.
In His presence, drawing what's needed, we emanate.

Acknowledging all our ways unto Him, in God we rejoice.
With paths made straight, we're freely given to His voice.
No matter how mundane, we submit freely to Him who sees all.
Developing a rhythm, we're no longer caught off guard.
Aligned with His purposes, our ways remain unmarred.

In humility, given to Him who redeems, we glorify.
No longer wise in our own eyes, we see through His eyes.
With the eyes of our understanding opened, He glorifies.
Embracing others in humility, we esteem as necessary.
Together in humility, we value one another as emissaries.

Fearing the Lord, shunning evil, He is glorified in our midst.
Our bodies strengthened; we mount up as eagles to assist.
In His fullness, fully equipped, we go in the power of His might.
Overflowing with blessings beyond measure, we invite.
Strengthened in the might of His Spirit, multitudes ignite.

With hearts to give of His wealth, His kingdom multiplies.
As His kingdom increases, draws are needed to supply.
In humility, honoring Him, we give freely as He directs.
Sowing in faith, He blesses and increases, filling exceedingly.
Blessings flowing freely, His glory fills all in all, unceasingly.

Prayer

Lord, help me remain humble in all that I do and say. As a lively stone, build me into all that You are doing.

~

May God bless you mightily as you humble yourself before Him. May He daily load you with benefits as ambassadors of His kingdom.

Day 24

Beware of Cultural Deception

With the vast majority of humankind blinded by the lies of the devil, our world is bound in deceit, which has given birth to the destruction that comes with it. As Christians, we must be aware of the cultural deception surrounding us, as the Psalmist warns us lest we become blinded by fool's wisdom.

Psalm 36:1-4 I have a message from God in my heart concerning the sinfulness of the wicked: there is no fear of God before their eyes. ² In their own eyes, they flatter themselves too much to detect or hate their sin. ³ The words of their mouths are wicked and deceitful; they fail to act wisely or do good. ⁴ Even on their beds, they plot evil; they commit themselves to a sinful course and do not reject what is wrong.

The Psalmist's message from God expresses the mass deception taking place in the cultures of the world today. In every arena of our societies, we experience what the Psalmist has to say in areas such as the entertainment industry, education system, government—both parties, economy, arts, media, religion, and family. Fool's wisdom is leading our world.

Cultural Deception and destruction have crept into the inner sanctuary of the Lord's house as well. Jesus intended His Church to be the pillar and ground of all truth. The Church is to be a place for the wisdom of God to flow out of rather than the wisdom of fools. Unfortunately, since truth has been replaced by the knowledge of fools, truth has fallen in the streets[74] with the cultures throughout our world lying in ruin and blinded by the

---

[74] Isaiah 59:14-15

devil's lies. With this in mind, Paul warns Timothy about the importance of how he should conduct himself as a preacher and teacher of God's word.

1 Timothy 3:15 But if I am delayed, I write to you so that you may know how you are to conduct yourself in the house of God, which is the church of the living God, the pillar and ground of the truth.

In the above passage, Paul urges his son in the faith, Timothy, the importance of conducting himself with absolute integrity towards the truth of God's word. Paul recognized the importance of maintaining absolute integrity when preaching God's word. He understood the responsibility given to the Church. **The Church is to be the pillar and ground of truth so that God can distill His truth throughout the world's cultures rather than fool's wisdom.** When the Church compromises and waters the truth down to make it more palatable, it opens the doors for fool's wisdom to creep in. James, the Lord's brother, goes so far as to say that teachers and preachers who do not maintain integrity towards God's word will receive a stricter judgment.[75]

When God's ambassadors do not boldly proclaim His unadulterated truth, justice turns back while righteousness stands afar off, resulting in God's people finding themselves prey.[76] Unfortunately, this is the predicament many Christians have fallen prey to in today's world. We live in dangerous times as the world turns against us as Christians. We can blame the devil all we want, but it is our

> Fool's wisdom is leading our world. It has even crept into the inner sanctuary of the Lord's house. Jesus intended His Church to be the pillar and ground of all truth. It is a place for the wisdom of God to flow out of rather than the wisdom of fools.

responsibility to restore truth in the streets by fearlessly proclaiming and living the truth of God's word with boldness and ferocity as deep darkness descends upon the world. During this season of darkness, it's time for His anointed ones to arise by allowing our lights to shine brightly in the manner the prophet Isaiah speaks prophetically of in the passage below.

Isaiah 60:1-2 Arise Shine; for your light has come! And the glory of the Lord is risen upon you. ² For behold, the darkness shall cover the earth, and deep darkness the people; but the Lord will arise over you, and His glory will be seen upon you.

---

[75] James 3:1
[76] Isaiah 59:14-15i

As we speak and act according to the wisdom flowing from above, it opens the doors for God's hidden knowledge to be glorified in our lives for all to see, hear, and sense. Because we have received that which comes from the Holy Spirit, He teaches us to compare spiritual things with spiritual. Making this comparison enables us not to get caught up in the foolish chatter of the world. He has given us the mind of Christ to keep us from the dangers of cultural deception as His Spirit searches the heart and wisdom of the Father in all things, even the deep things of God.[77]

May God help us all not to get swept up in the cultural deception of our times. Satan is on a rampage to steal, kill, and destroy the truths that will set people free from their bondage to cultural addictions of every kind. We must allow God's word to be our filter in all we do and speak. In doing so, we will stand firm against the lies and schemes of the enemy. Know that difficult times are upon us. This season is not a time to walk in self-deception and the wisdom of this age, but rather a time to become fools for Christ that we may become wise in God and His ways.[78]

***2 Timothy 3:1-5** But know this that in the last days perilous times will come: ² For men will be lovers of themselves, lovers of money, boasters, proud, blasphemers, disobedient to parents, unthankful, unholy, ³ unloving, unforgiving, slanderers, without self-control, brutal, despisers of good, ⁴ traitors, headstrong, haughty, lovers of pleasure rather than lovers of God. ⁵ Having a form of godliness but denying its power. And from such people turn away!"*

Poem: Blinded by Fool's Wisdom

Given to forbidden fruit, eyes wide open, we trip and stumble.
With eyes all-embracing, much of what's seen is an illusion.
Caught up in false paradigms of thinking, we run to gain.
Trapped in distorted realities, we walk in fool's wisdom.
Tripping through life, all that's sensed is not as it seems.

Blinded by the gods of this world, we trip and stumble.
Ignoring the gentle voice of reasoning, we press to gain.
Caught up in collective reasoning, we spit venom recklessly.
As the web of deceit spreads, violence advances rapidly.
Lost in false illusions, the collective mindset prevails.

As reason disappears, violence induces masses to insanity.
Blinded by failed ideologies, we stumble about in fool's wisdom.

---

[77] 1 Corinthians 2:6-10
[78] 1 Corinthians 3:18-19

The Rise of the Anointed Ones – Beware of Cultural Deception

Looking around, eyes sweeping, questions rising, we listen.
Gazing at the fires of destruction, we stand beleaguered.
As freedom discards, in pain and turmoil, we trip and stumble.

Searching for meaning, coming up short, fools prevail.
Standing in shadows of the unseen, we're left reaching.
With hearts crying out in pain, we question all that's seen.
As fire and destruction rage on, we're left wondering.
Is there hope in the midst of all that's disparaging?

Given to inflated idealism, with lies propagated, we misstep.
As truth falls in the streets, will it once again be restored?
Will the Church arise in glory with its pillars of truth in place?
Will we take responsibility for our self-will and deception?
Will we open our eyes to the still, small voice, long forgotten?

Let us rise from the ash heaps of self-destruction and compel.
Let us put away our false ideologies, allowing truth to prevail.
Let us disregard collective reasoning and put on the mind of Christ.
Let us partake of the wisdom from above rather than fool's wisdom.
Let us return to our first love, being kind to those of other mindsets.

Prayer

Lord, help me not fall prey to all that is going on in our world today. Teach me to keep my focus on all that You are doing rather than the evil influences around me. Lead me away from the traps Satan tries to set in my way. Help me be among those whose lights shine brightly amid the darkness that is beginning to cover the earth.

~

May God bless you mightily as He leads you away from Satan's lies and traps, allowing you to shine brightly amid the cultural deception.

Day 25

Restoring Truth To the Streets

Without the acknowledgment of God, who is the source of all truth, there is no such thing as truth. There are no absolutes. Truth becomes whatever is suitable for the individual, which is nothing more than a mixture of lies and half-truths weaved into the fabric of our societies and cultures to create confusion from the father of lies. As a result, our world lies in ruins because of a lack of justice. As the prophet says, righteousness stands afar off.

Isaiah 59:14 Justice is turned back, and righteousness stands afar off; for truth has stumbled in the streets, and equity cannot enter.

When addressing the religious leaders and Pharisees, Jesus referred to their teachings as a mixture of their ideas with what Moses had taught them.

Matthew 15;1-6 Then the scribes and Pharisees who were from Jerusalem came to Jesus, saying, ² "Why do Your disciples transgress the tradition of the elders? For they do not wash their hands when they eat bread." ³ He answered and said to them, "Why do you also transgress the commandment of God because of your tradition? ⁴ For God commanded, saying, 'Honor your father and your mother'; and, 'He who curses father or mother, let him be put to death.' ⁵ But you say, 'Whoever says to his father or mother, "Whatever profit you might have received from me is a gift to God"— ⁶ then he need not honor his father or mother.' Thus you have made the commandment of God of no effect by your tradition.

Absolute truth gets ignored because people would rather feed their carnal desires than embrace God's truth. If we want to avoid the father of lies, we must embrace wholeheartedly the uncompromising truth that comes from all Scripture given by the inspiration of God through holy men who were moved on by the Holy Spirit.[79] As we uncompromisingly welcome the truth, it enables us to be vessels of honor as we go into the harvest fields of the Lord that are already white for harvest.

2 Timothy 3:16-17 All Scripture is given by inspiration of God *and is profitable for doctrine, for reproof, for correction, for instruction in righteousness* [17] *that the man of God may be complete, thoroughly equipped for every good work.*

When Jesus came before Pilate, He had an interesting conversation concerning truth. Some might think Pilate was being facetious, but he was serious. Without being connected to the source of truth and the absolutes that come from it, truth is a very nebulous thing. What constitutes truth? Is it Power? Rome was the nation of power during this time of history and therefore dictated what truth was. Without the authority of the Scriptures, there is no truth. It's up for grabs to whoever has the most vital voice. Everyone becomes right in their own eyes, believing the lies that spill forth out of the pits of hell from the father of lies, Satan. These are lies spilled out into the streets of our world today that have caused the truth of God's word to have fallen in the streets.

> Truth becomes whatever is suitable for the individual, which is nothing more than a mixture of lies and half-truths weaved into the fabric of our societies and cultures to create confusion from the father of lies.

The voices of the antichrist spirit are alive and well, screaming blatantly with force in today's world. The enemies of our faith are bullying Christians into believing the lies spilling out into the streets of the world.

It's time for Christians everywhere to take a stand for the truth of God's word by putting on the belt of truth, which is a significant part of our spiritual armor. We must quit compromising the truths we know for the sake of being accepted in the world's eyes. Even though we may become prey to those who speak forth the lies of their father, the devil, we must restore the pillars of truth so that truth will spill out into the streets rather than the lies of the antichrist spirit. We will not restore truth and equity to our cultures, which lie in ruin, until Christians everywhere take a stand for God's word by seriously obeying it and having their steps ordered by it. Our adherence to God's word will bring forth light amid darkness and cause us to be living epistles to all those swayed and captured by the enemy's lies and deceit.

---

[79] 2 Peter 1:21

The Rise of the Anointed Ones – Restoring Truth to the Streets

1 Timothy 3:15 *I write to you so that you may know how you ought to conduct yourself in the House of God,* **which is the church of the living God, the pillar and ground of the truth.**

As seen from the above Scripture, the Church is the answer the world is looking for to solve its problems. Unfortunately, the world doesn't know because the Church has compromised itself with the mixture of the world. Those caught up in the lies of Satan cannot understand what truth is because they have not been adequately exposed to the purity of truth that should be flowing from the Church of the living God, the pillar and ground of all truth. It's time for the Church of the living God to wake up to the uncompromising truth of God's word and walk in it as He has commanded us to do. Therefore, the apostle John writes, *"I have no greater joy than to hear that my children are walking in truth."*[80] We have been anointed for such a time. We have entered into a season for God's anointed ones to rise.

> Those caught up in the lies of Satan can't understand what truth is because they haven't been adequately exposed to the purity of truth that should be flowing from the Church of the living God.

What kind of a mixture are you walking in today? Are you ready to take a stand for truth? You must decide for yourself if you're going to embrace the entirety of God's word without compromise or walk in the half-truths that Satan mixes with lies. It is only the truth of God's word that will set you free. We must all determine to be like the Bereans, who searched the Scriptures daily to make sure what they were hearing was accurate.[81] We must awaken from our slumber and arm ourselves with the belt of truth if we are to restore truth to the streets of our cities. May we all band together under the armor of God's holy word as He sends revival our way.

Poem: Awakened from Slumber

In an era of declining morals, gates open wide for immorality.
Reveling in his lustful ways, Satan comes taking advantage.
Caught in the tide of wickedness, God's people become prey.
Like a roaring lion, he comes devouring and exploiting lies.
As truth lies dead in the streets, cultures crumble before our eyes.

God's word tossed aside like pieces of cardboard, sin flourishes.
His word no longer a measurement, His authority diminishes.

---

[80] 3 John 1:4
[81] Acts 17:11

The Rise of the Anointed Ones – Restoring Truth to the Streets

With authority undercut, the bulwark of truth gives way to the tide.
As the pillars of truth begin to crumble, Satan is emboldened.
Unleashing his venom, those who oppose are misrepresented.

As Satan's fury unleashes, compromise enters the ranks.
Seeking to be relevant in fear of losing, the Church weakens.
No longer standing strong, authority diminishes as sin creeps in.
Caught in a web of unbelief, the enemy comes, sowing tares.
No longer discernible between wheat and tares, she loses voice.

Asleep in the darkness, we awaken to our condition.
Putting on the armor of light, we begin mending our ways.
Bold as a lion, in His righteousness, we roar with realization.
Standing in the gap, the pillars of truth, we begin to restore.
Embracing the sovereignty of our Lord, we build with vigor.

Looking sin, squarely in the eyes, a commitment is made.
No longer compromising, we repent, having strayed.
Proclaiming righteousness, we preach, no longer afraid.
Calling God's people to repent from all sin, we plead.
Aligned with God's word and sovereignty, we lead.

Identity and morals fully restored; we embrace restoration.
Ready and willing, a workman, unashamed, we strengthen.
Fully submitting to His sovereignty, with Jesus, we co-labor.
With the pillars of truth back in place, His Church, we rebuild.
With gates fully restored, Satan's ploys are quickly quelled.

The Chief Cornerstone in place, the building He fitly frames.
Coming to the stature of Christ's fullness, evil no longer inflames.
Receiving a double portion, we go forth in the power of His Spirit.
As glory fills, He ushers in multitudes before the curtain falls.
Awakened from slumber, we stand fully girded for the final battle.

Prayer

Lord, give me the heart to know the uncompromising truth of Your word.
Challenge me to let go of the compromised areas in my life.

~

May the blessing of God be on you as you walk in the truth of God's word without compromise.

Day 26

The Bride of Christ Revealed

Throughout the Scriptures, God paints a beautiful picture in our imaginations of the relationship between Christ and His Bride. As we give ourselves to His paintbrush, we can picture in our minds the bride, He is preparing for His only begotten Son, who will appear in the glory and splendor of her Lord as she awaits His Coming.

Revelation 19:7 *Let us be glad and rejoice and give Him glory, for the marriage of the Lamb has come, and His wife has made herself ready.*

The picture the Father reveals to us is one in which the bride of Christ plays a significant role in all that God desires to do before the coming of the great day of the Lord. With His brush, the Father paints a remarkable picture. She is the centerpiece of His prophetic purposes for the end of the age. She is the star of the end-time scenario. Because we are the members in particular who make up the bride of Christ, we need to know what the Lord's purposes are and what our roles are in relationship to all that God desires to do before Christ's second coming. We are the bride of Christ.

In Matthew's gospel, after Jesus finished sharing with His disciples about the signs of the end of the age, He gave them parables to illustrate how we are to prepare for all that is about to come upon us. The first parable is the "Parable of the Ten Virgins."[82] This parable illustrates the importance of being ready for all that God is about to do before the second coming of Christ. Under the inspiration of the Holy Spirit, Matthew uses the term "Virgins" to define the bride of Christ's relationship to her espoused husband, the Lord Jesus Christ. Paul writes that she will be presented as a

---

[82] Matthew 25:1-10

The Rise of the Anointed Ones – The Bride of Christ Revealed

chaste virgin to Christ in one of his letters.[83] Next, Matthew uses the term "Oil" to illustrate the anointing of the Holy Spirit,[84] which is necessary to carry out the purposes of God. The Lamps represent God's word as it unfolds in our lives to help guide us. As it says in Psalms, *"Your word is a lamp to my feet and a light to my path."*[85]

The parable of "The Ten Virgins" illustrates how the oil and the lamp work together to make us ready to meet our bridegroom. The lamp without the oil would be useless in the same way the oil without the lamp would be. As the oil represents the Holy Spirit's anointing in our lives and the lamp represents the word of God, we see the importance of how God's word and the Spirit partner together to make us ready. It's our responsibility to make sure this happens. As we continually read and study God's word, we must ask the Holy Spirit to enlighten our understanding as we go forth in the power of His anointing to accomplish the tasks the Father gave us.

We find another beautiful picture of the bride of Christ in chapter twelve of the book of Revelation. Here we see a picture of the bride after she comes into the fullness of the stature of Christ, which is significant part of the prophetic purposes that must be fulfilled before Jesus returns. In this passage, she is portrayed or clothed in her wedding garments; the sun, the moon, and the stars representing the fullness of the Godhead bodily.[86] She's fully clothed in the Lord Jesus Christ, which name represents the fullness of the Godhead bodily. Dressed in her wedding garments, she has now been made ready for the great marriage.[87]

Revelation 12:1 *Now a great sign appeared in heaven; a woman clothed with the sun, with the moon under her feet, and on her head a garland of twelve stars.*

During the period of the trumpet judgments in the book of Revelation, she leads the world into the greatest spiritual harvest of souls known to humanity, a period in which the Spirit and the bride say, "Come!"[88] Then, with the fulfillment of Ezekiel's prophecy of the dry bones unfolding, she arises in the fullness of the stature of Christ and fulfills the prophecy of Jesus when He said; we will do greater works than He did.[89] Finally, with the great Day of Atonement fulfilled, she is ready to be swept away on the

---

[83] 2 Corinthians 11:2
[84] 1 John 2:20, 27, the word anointing means to smear with oil.
[85] Psalm 119:105
[86] Romans 1:20
[87] Revelation 19:7
[88] Revelation 22:17
[89] Ephesians 4:13

wings of a great eagle to partake in the fulfillment of the Feast of Tabernacles for the final three and one-half years of the great tribulation during the rule of the antichrist.[90] The wilderness is a special place of protection where God will nourish the bride of Christ from the presence of Satan during the final plagues of God's wrath as the bowl of judgments mentioned in Revelation 16 pour out by the seven angels. It is where she is kept or escapes from the hour of trial, which shall come upon the whole earth.[91]

Revelation 3:10 *Because you have kept My command to persevere, I will also keep you from the hour of trial which shall come upon the whole world to test those who dwell on the earth.*

In the same way, God protected the nation of Israel during the ten plagues of judgment and brought them into the wilderness, so He does again in this great exodus. Isaiah illustrates this perfectly when he speaks of the seven women who take hold of one man to remove their reproach. The number seven speaks of perfection. She comes into her fullness as the Branch of the Lord is now beautiful and glorious. God ushers her into the Feast of Tabernacles, where He creates above every dwelling place a cloud of smoke by day and flaming fire by night. This place is a shelter from the storm or tribulation.[92] The Scriptures also refer to Her place of escape as her bridal chambers. God hides her here until the indignation, or the tribulation is over.[93]

As we draw closer and closer to the end time environment mentioned in Scripture, we must gather ourselves together as His bride and prepare for the great harvest of souls that is to take place during this period.

Zephaniah 2:1-3 *Gather yourselves together, O undesirable nation, ² before the decree is issued, or the day passes like chaff, before the Lord's fierce anger comes upon you, before the day of the Lord's anger comes upon you! ³ Seek the Lord, all you meek of the earth, who have upheld justice. Seek righteousness, seek humility. It may be that you will be hidden in the day of the Lord's anger.*

Now is the time to receive the extra supply of oil that separates the wise virgins from the foolish virgins left behind to face the antichrist's wrath. Many foolish virgins or Christians will fall away during this time, known as *"The great falling away."* The Antichrist martyrs them because they

---

[90] Isaiah 4:1-3
[91] Revelation 3:10, Isaiah 26:17, 20-21, Zephaniah 2:1-3
[92] Isaiah 4:1-6,
[93] Isaiah 26:17-18, 20-21

won't submit to his control by taking the mark.[94] When the Bride of Christ is rescued and taken to her place of safety, the restraining power of the Holy Spirit leaves. The antichrist is then free and without restraint to blaspheme God and set up his throne.[95]

I know this is a very sobering thought, but we must allow the truth of God's word to set us free to pursue the anointing needed to fill our lamps. The fear of God is the beginning of wisdom that helps to qualify us as wise virgins. We will need that extra supply of oil to shine brightly for all to see as we go forth as Christ's bride warning and gathering in a harvest of souls during the period leading up to the great tribulation.

May God bless you richly as you meditate on all that God is about to do. May you have ears to hear what the Holy Spirit is saying in this critical hour of the Church's destiny. [96]

~

For a complete and thorough study on this subject, please see my book, "Prophetic Purposes and the Zeal of the Lord," – booksbyken.com.

Poem: The Bride of Christ Revealed

Clothed in beauty and splendor, her Lord crowns her.
Moving about, she spreads His fragrance everywhere.
Crowned with stars, as a royal diadem, she shines brightly.
Espoused as a chaste virgin to her love, she waits nightly.
As angels above rejoice, she awaits her chariot.

In faithfulness, she takes hold of Him, who takes her shame.
Standing in His righteousness, she takes on His name.
By the spirit of judgment and burning, she's purged now waiting.
With her filth washed away, she's made excellent and appealing.
Without spot or blemish, in holiness, she awaits her bridegroom.

Toiling day and night as a virtuous woman, she prepares.
Standing firmly on her foundation, His radiance, she declares.
As the moon reflects the sun, she radiates her Father's grandeur.

---

[94] 2 Thessalonians 2:3-7, Revelation 13:7-8: 20:4
[95] 2 Thessalonians 2:6-7
[96] For a more exhaustive study on this subject, please check out my book, "Prophetic Purposes and the Zeal of the Lord."

The Rise of the Anointed Ones – The Bride of Christ Revealed

As multitudes await this great day, others mock and ignore.
As the wedding day nears, the Spirit and bride say, come.

Impregnated by the Spirit, she awaits the birth of her male child.
Gathering herself together, the decree is about to be unveiled.
Hoping to be hidden from the Master's wrath, she seeks and waits.
Toiling and waiting as a wise virgin, she fills her lamps with oil.
As her Master measures the temple, He finds her measure full.

Giving birth to her male child, the enemy tries to snatch him.
Before he's snatched, he's caught up to heaven above.
Now angry, Satan makes war with this beautiful bride as prey.
Quickly rescued from a tide of violence, she's swept away.
Arriving in the form of an eagle, her chariot gives her ride.

Taken to her bridal chambers, she dwells in safety from the storm.
Allured to a unique place in the wilderness, she awaits her bridegroom.
The Father's fury now ready; it unleashes on all who dwell on earth.
Safely hidden away, she rests in her shelter from the storm.
She wonders, "What happens to our little sister, the foolish virgins?"

Caught up to her Bridegroom, the Father's fury is about to end.
Received and known as He is, her marriage now consummates.
Her groom, riding on a white horse, gathers saints to encounter.
Gathered from the four winds for battle, they're prepared.
With the brightness of His coming, those left on earth are scorched.

Those caught up, live and reign with Christ, attending a great banquet.
From every generation, saints with the Patriarchs come to sup.
A thousand years of peace, they build, plant, and rule nations.
Loosed for a short season; Satan deceives again as the great pretender.
With the new earth and heavens, the bride appears in glorious splendor.[97]

Prayer

Father, I pray You fill my lamp with oil so that those in my pathways will be touched.

---

[97] Scripture references: Revelation 12:1, 2 Corinthians 2:15, 11:2, Proverbs 31:10-31, Revelation 19:7, Isaiah 4:1, 4, 62:3-5, Ephesians 5:27, Romans 1:20, Psalm 84:11, Zephaniah 2:1-3, Joel 3:14, Revelation 11:1-2, Matthew 25:1-13, Revelation 12:4-6, 14, Isaiah 26:17, 20-21, 4:4-6, Revelation 13:7, 20:4, 1 Thessalonians 4:17, 1 Corinthians 15:52, 1 John 3:2, Revelation 19:11-16.

Day 27

Fervency on Demand

We should ask ourselves, what will it take to increase our fervency level? First, let's think about what it means to be fervent in the Spirit for a moment. Some choice words that describe fervency are intense, enthusiastic, emotional, wholehearted, dedicated, and animated. These words give us a good perspective of what it means when encouraged through Scripture not to lag in fervency as Paul encouraged us.

Romans 12:11 *Not lagging in diligence, fervent in spirit, serving the Lord.*

Fervency is something that is lacking in much of today's Christianity. It appears many are more interested in exploring their liberties in Christ than embracing the cross of Christ, which leads to a sacrificial life of fervently serving the Lord with diligence. The Father's heart towards us is that we would be fervent in the Spirit as we willingly embrace the grace of God that leads us away from worldly desires and the lusts of the flesh that war against the Spirit within us.

Fervency involves all the above words that describe it, plus having or showing great warmth or intensity of spirit with a feeling of enthusiasm. Does this describe your walk with God? It should! If you are like most people, it comes and goes depending on your circumstances. Our goal is to remain vibrant no matter what hardships, trials, and temptations we may face. An excellent example for us to consider is when Paul and Silas found themselves in jail for preaching the gospel while in Philippi. While chained and in prison, they expressed their level of zeal by praying and singing hymns to God. As a result, the Lord worked with them mightily, causing an earthquake, resulting in the jailer and his family getting saved and water baptized.[98] The kingdom advanced because of Paul and Silas'

---

[98] Acts 16:25-34

The Rise of the Anointed Ones – Fervency on Demand

level of enthusiasm. Is the kingdom of God advancing because of our level of zeal, or are we just ho-hum about it?

The challenge for all of us is to maintain our fervency level in all seasons and circumstances no matter what our circumstances are. It's easy to be fervent when everything is going well. The tricky question is, how do we respond to the seasons when it seems like God pulls a disappearing act and nothing goes right? We must be like Job, who said, *"Thou He slay me, I will trust in Him and maintain my ways."*[99]

When Paul mentions we are not to lag in diligence, he urges us to keep our zeal by focusing our minds on the appeal he made to the Colossians when he said, *"To this end, I also labor, striving according to His working, which works in me mightily."* Paul reminds us that the Holy Spirit within us works mightily on our behalf. Paul understood he was a partner with the Holy Spirit, which caused him to work mightily alongside Him. Working

> Those who are dedicated and passionate in their faith, despite their circumstances, take the kingdom by force.

alongside the Holy Spirit helped Paul maintain his fervency level while suffering for Christ and pursuing the Lord's calling in his life. When we fail to strive according to the Holy Spirit's working in our lives, we quench what He desires to do in and through us, which causes our level of enthusiasm to dissipate. Therefore, Paul warns us, *"Do not quench the Spirit."*[100]

Paul went through many seasons that weren't all that pleasant, yet he kept his level of fervency high during the worst of them. After almost being stoned to death on one occasion, he urged the disciples to continue in the faith, saying, *"We must through many tribulations enter the kingdom of God."*[101] Our seasons of discomfort won't come close to what Paul experienced, yet we seem to give up so easily amid trials and hardships. We tend to revert to worldly things to comfort our souls instead of remaining fervent in the spirit. But, as Paul wrote to young Timothy, we must endure hardships as good soldiers of Jesus Christ.[102] Those who are dedicated and passionate in their faith, despite their circumstances, take the kingdom by force.

---

[99] Job 13:15
[100] 1 Thessalonians 5:19
[101] Acts 14:22
[102] 2 Timothy 2:3

The kingdom of God has been suffering violent attacks from the enemy in every stratum of society known to humanity. It's time for the anointed ones to rise during all the turmoil and destruction Satan has caused. God has destined us to take the kingdom by force with enthusiasm and zeal that will quell the enemy's devices.[103] We must be fervent in the spirit under all circumstances for this to happen. Let's be like Paul and strive according to the Holy Spirit's working, who desires to work mightily in us.

***Ephesians 1:19-20** And what is the exceeding greatness of His power toward us who believe, according to the working of His mighty power [20] which He worked in Christ when He raised Him from the dead and seated Him at His right hand in the heavenly places.*

People whose hearts are fully committed to God's purposes will rise in the anointing with enthusiasm to the challenge all that they can be in Christ with His power working in them mightily. May God bless you greatly as you rise in the anointing to the challenge!

Poem: Vehement Desire Unleashed

Led by the Spirit, baptized into His fullness, we engage.
Not lagging in diligence, fervency catapults forward.
Knowing the Lord works mightily in us, we press on.
Amid trials and temptations, we stand firm in the faith.
Not giving in to selfish desires, we serve God diligently.

Denying worldly lusts, vehement desire takes hold.
Embracing the cross sacrificially, we give of ourselves.
In wholehearted, dedicated, commitment, passion explodes.
Pursuing destiny, gifts explode into action, releasing power.
Partnering with the Holy Spirit, vehement desire unleashes.

Taking the kingdom by force with earnest desire, we rule.
Quelling the enemy's devices, passion paves the way.
With strongholds torn down, the kingdom advances.
As the kingdom advances, many join the pursuit.
Filled with a spirit of unity, His zeal spreads rapidly.

Taking His word seriously, hearts fill with expectation.
Knowing there are prophecies to be fulfilled, we stand ready.
Responding to His command, zeal ignites into explosive action.

---

[103] Matthew 11:12

With sincere desire exploding into action, His Spirit releases.
As healings, miracles, prophetic words release, He gathers.

With the culmination of all things at hand, He fills all in all.
As His glory spreads over the earth, those gathered wait.
Blinded by deceit, those standing in resistance writhe in pain.
Incapable of understanding, their senses destroyed, they cry.
As Satan spews, the Spirit of the Lord delivers just in time.

Prayer

Father God, help me keep my eyes focused on You, even during times of hardship. Help me never to lack diligence and enthusiasm as I give myself to your purposes. Help me always be aware of the assignments You have given me so that Your name will be glorified in all that I do.

~

May God bless and anoint you mightily as you strive according to the Holy Spirit working in you mightily to be all you can be in Christ.

Day 28

Kingdom Perspectives that Transform

Do you find the decisions you make concerning your life work out for good, or do you often regret the choices you've made? The temptation for all of us is to fall into the trap of humanistic thinking. But God has given us the mind of Christ to plan our ways rather than our idealistic thoughts.

Proverbs 19:21 *(NIV) Many are the plans in a man's heart, but it is the Lord's purpose that prevails.*

Because we are carnal beings, we have thinking processes that come naturally to us. But God has a different plan. He desires for us to be spiritually minded. Because His ways and thoughts are so much higher than ours, it takes a spiritual mind to be in sync with Him. To be carnally minded goes against His plans for our lives. Being spiritually minded brings us into His kingdom perspectives that can transform our lives from the mundane into a life governed by the supernatural, which continually adds new dimensions to our way of thinking.

Romans 8:5-7 *For those who live according to the flesh set their minds on things of the flesh, but those who live according to the Spirit, the things of the Spirit. ⁶ For to be carnally minded is death, but to be spiritually minded is life and peace. ⁷ Because the carnal mind is enmity against God; for it is not subject to the law of God, nor indeed can be.*

When our self-centered thoughts and ways govern our lives, we are at war with God and cannot expect things to turn out right. As a result, we become schemers and manipulators to get what we want rather than depending on Him and His ways and means to work things out. On the other hand, when we are spiritually minded, we are governed by His kingdom purposes. As kingdom-minded men and women, we then make our decisions and choices from a kingdom perspective that transforms us into the image of Christ and move us forward into the destiny and purposes God mapped out for us as shown in the passage below.

Psalm 139:16-17 *My frame was not hidden from You when I was made in secret and skillfully wrought in the lowest parts of the earth.* *[16] Your eyes saw my substance, being yet unformed.* *[17] And in Your book, they were all written, the days fashioned for me, when as yet they were none of them.*

As Spiritually minded people, we base our decisions in life on God's overall mission and purposes and the destiny to which He called us to, rather our selfish ambitions and desires for the moment. In other words, we seek first the kingdom of God in all things. By submitting our deliberations to God, we discover His blessings freely flow as He imparts all things pertaining unto life and godliness. Therefore, when we purpose to seek God with our whole hearts, we find ourselves submitting to Him, even the most mundane of things as well as our significant decisions. In doing so, we acknowledge God in all our ways.

> Spiritually minded people base their decisions in life on God's overall mission and purposes and the destiny to which God called them to, rather than their selfish ambitions and desires for the moment.

He, then, can lead us into the destiny He wrote in His book.[104] On the other hand, carnally minded people constantly chafe at the bit and frustrate the grace of God, thus missing the destiny He marked out for them.

Matthew 6:33 *But seek first the kingdom of God and His righteousness, and all these things will be added unto you.*

Leading up to the above passage, Jesus encouraged His disciples not to worry about food, clothing, or shelter. As long as they sought the kingdom of God first, the Heavenly Father would take care of their needs. Seeking Jesus and His kingdom first is a primary attribute belonging to kingdom people who desire God to use them. When our lives are so weighed down with worry or concern in trying to make ends meet, we make poor decisions and have little energy for the prophetic purposes of God. We must learn to trust in His ability to take care of us as we give ourselves wholeheartedly as we tend to the Father's business. By doing so, He makes our paths straight when we lean into His understanding rather than our carnal ways of thinking.

---

[104] Proverbs 3:5-6

The Rise of the Anointed Ones – Kingdom Perspectives that Transform

Proverbs 3:5-6 *(NIV) Trust in the Lord with all your heart and lean not on your own understanding; ⁶ in all your ways submit to him, and he will make your paths straight.*

Submission or acknowledging implies submitting to God and His ways continually. Our relationship with the Lord entails submitting to His thoughts and ways because He sees us from an eternal perspective. Having already seen our future, He knows what's ahead and plans our courses accordingly. As we freely submit our ways unto Him, He can direct our steps accordingly. The more submitted we are, the more of His grace and excellence we experience. As a result, we continually walk in the transformation process and are changed from glory to glory into the image of Christ with the destiny He has charted out for us.

Poem: From Despondency to Hope

Trusting in our own ways, we plan and scheme.
Filled with self-gloating and rejoicing, we daydream.
Given to self-centered, appealing choices, we squander.
Reaping what was sown, the mind begins to wander.
Wallowing in regret and remorse, our choices, we ponder.

Reaping a life governed by self, we stand demoralized.
Caught in self-loathing, repercussions come our way.
Disenchanted, the soul weighed down in regret, we fret.
In depression, anxiety, and suicidal thoughts, we dismay.
Giving into the bitterness of the moment, we cry for relief.

Caught in webs of hopelessness, we look for a ray of light.
In the distance, a light beckons for further exploration.
Intrigued, a glimmer of hope penetrates areas unknown.
As the light penetrates, despair begins to dissolve.
Lifted from despair, heartened by the light, hope resolves.

Heartened and hopeful, we immerse ourselves in the light.
Looking for new direction, we readily discard old mindsets.
As light penetrates areas of the heart, a gentle voice beckons.
Becoming clearer, the voice beckons to the invisible glimpsed.
Excitement taking over, weights lift with new perceptions.

Discovering an invisible kingdom, we give ourselves freely.
The voice revealed as the kingdom's King, we follow readily.
No longer filled with fear, hate, and suicidal thoughts, we press.
Allowing the King's purposes to lead, new strategies, we envision.
The heart fully engaged, we commit to His ways and decisions.

The Rise of the Anointed Ones – Kingdom Perspectives that Transform

Choices, now governed by kingdom perspectives, we thrive.
Enhanced by fresh revelation, taken into deeper realms, we dive.
Guided by wisdom, kingdom choices produce peaceful solutions.
Given to mission and purpose, we delight in all that's gained.
As hope fills, we no longer wander, disenchanted with life.

Prayer

Heavenly Father, I come before You today, asking for wisdom and direction in all that I do. Fill my heart with Your wisdom and revelation of who You are and how You desire to work in my life today. I commit my day to You and acknowledge You in all my ways as I deal with whatever comes my way. Help me not to lean on my understanding.

~

As you embrace the kingdom perspectives that will transform your life into a faithful follower of Christ, may these perspectives be the guiding influence of your life along with the leading of the Holy Spirit.

Day 29

Avoiding Worldliness At All Costs

Kevin DeYoung is quoted as saying, *"Worldliness is whatever makes sin look normal and righteousness look strange."* In our minds, how do we view sin? Have the world's sinful ways become normal to us while righteousness and holiness seem foreign? If so, we need to consider what the beloved disciple has to say concerning worldliness.

I John 2:15-17 Do not love the world or the things in the world. If anyone loves the world, the love of the Father is not in him. [16] For all that is in the world—the lust of the flesh, the lust of the eyes, and the pride of life—is not of the Father but is of the world. [17] And the world is passing away, and the lust of it; but he who does the will of God abides forever.

We live in an era in which the morals of the world and the Church are rapidly declining. The Bible, God's Holy word, is no longer the authority by which we measure morality in our cultures. The Church has watered down and compromised the truth, so much so that its authority has eroded significantly. The Church is no longer the pillar and ground of all truth that stands as a bulwark against the tide of sinful and wicked behavior. Our cultures have given way to the surge of wickedness and immoral behavior washing up against its shores. Satan uses the lusts of the flesh, the lust of the eyes, and the pride of life to destroy everything in sight as sinful and worldly behaviors run freely without boundaries. The collective conscience of our cultures has become seared. For God-fearing Christians, we must avoid worldliness at all costs, lest our consciences become seared as well.

Our hope is found in Jesus Christ and adhering to the authority of Scripture if we are to save ourselves and those who hear us. Without God's word as an authority to measure our lives, anything and everything becomes acceptable behavior, which could cause Christianity to get swept up in the tide of that's washing up against the shores of humankind as well.

Satan, has sown tares in the world's harvest fields to the degree that it's hard to tell the difference between wheat and tares.[105] Spiritual deception is rampant in the Christian world today as a result. Newborn babes in Christ hardly stand a chance against the wiles of the devil because the Church as a whole has become so compromised when it comes to sin and worldliness. A little leaven has leavened the whole lump. As Paul wrote to the Corinthians, the old leaven must be purged. He said, *"Therefore purge out the old leaven, that you may be a new lump, since you truly are unleavened. For indeed, Christ, our Passover, was sacrificed for us. Therefore, let us keep the feast, not with old leaven, nor with the leaven of malice and wickedness, but with the unleavened bread of sincerity and truth."* [106]

> The Church needs to wake up to the fact that the leaven of sin and wickedness must be purged. Rather than turning a blind eye and pretending it doesn't exist amongst its ranks, we must look it squarely in the eye and see the damage it has caused.

The Church needs to wake up to the fact that the leaven of sin and wickedness must be purged. Rather than turning a blind eye and pretending it doesn't exist amongst its ranks, we must look it squarely in the eye and see the damage it has caused. Every born-again Christian has the responsibility before God to purge the sin in their lives and not conform to worldly thinking and carnal behavior as the following Scriptures encourage us to do.

Ephesians 4:21-24 if indeed you have heard Him and have been taught by Him, as the truth is in Jesus: [22] that you put off, concerning your former conduct, the old man which grows corrupt according to the deceitful lusts, [23] and be renewed in the spirit of your mind, [24] and that you put on the new man which was created according to God, in true righteousness and holiness.

1 Corinthians 6:9-11 Do you not know that the unrighteous will not inherit the kingdom of God? Do not be deceived. Neither fornicators, nor idolaters, nor adulterers, nor homosexuals, nor sodomites, [10] nor thieves, nor covetous, nor drunkards, nor revilers, nor extortioners will inherit the kingdom of God. [11] And

---

[105] Matthew 13:24-30
[106] Galatians 5:9, 1 Corinthians 5:6-7

The Rise of the Anointed Ones – Avoiding Worldliness at all Costs

such were some of you. But you were washed, but you were sanctified, but you were justified in the name of the Lord Jesus and by the Spirit of our God.

Most of the sinful behavior mentioned in the above passage is now normal behavior in our cultures today. However, God's holy word is timeless, meaning as Christians, we should not have our values dictated by cultural norms. God's word and values remain constant. God, who sees the past, present, and future in His omniscience, breathed the Scriptures into existence through holy men of God as the Holy Spirit moved on them. So likewise, He saw our present-day as He breathed these Scriptures into existence.[107] In other words, God inspired the above passage of Scripture with a complete understanding of what our cultures would look like in our day. His word is timeless and is meant for us, just as it was for the disciples of the first century.

We must separate from those caught up in the spirit of the world and cleanse ourselves from all filthiness of the flesh and spirit. We are encouraged to avoid worldliness at all costs lest we be guilty of spiritual adultery.[108] Instead, we are to humble ourselves before God, who gives more grace to those who come before Him in humility. He yearns jealousy on our behalf. Let us not be a part of all that in unclean as we put on the new nature birthed out of God's righteousness rather than the world's uncleanness. We must resist and avoid the squeeze of the world at all costs.

2 Corinthians 6:16-7:1 "And what agreement has the temple of God with idols? For you are the temple of the living God. As God has said: "I will dwell in them and walk among them. I will be their God, and they shall be My people." 17 Therefore, "Come out from among them and be separate, says the Lord. Do not touch what is unclean, and I will receive you." 18 "I will be a Father to you, and you shall be My sons and daughters, says the LORD Almighty." 7:1 "Therefore, having these promises, beloved, let us cleanse ourselves from all filthiness of the flesh and spirit, perfecting holiness in fear of God."

Poem: Righteousness in a Contaminated World

Destructive ways, tearing down cultures, Satan contaminates.
Seeking to destroy all in his path, he has no concern for life.
Coming as a liar and a deceiver, the righteous, he attacks.

---

[107] 2 Peter1:21, 2 Timothy 3:16
[108] James 4:4-10

The Rise of the Anointed Ones – Avoiding Worldliness at all Costs

Knowing his time is short, he comes with a vengeance.
Usurping authority from above, he proclaims himself as God.

As a tide of wickedness sweeps upon our shores, fear arises.
Amid Satan's treachery, the Father calls for moral excellence.
Called to stand firm in courage, we take heed to ourselves.
Forsaking worldly entanglements, we become strong in grace.
Denying lust and things of the world, moral excellence reigns.

Allowing Word and Spirit to guide, we gain grace and strength.
Exhorted to be strong in the grace of God, we become pillars.
With pillars in place, we stand as a bulwark against the tide.
As righteousness gains a foothold, his attacks lose strength.
Called to be holy as He is, we clothe ourselves in His virtue.

As His lights amid darkness, we become beacons of hope.
Though contaminated with treachery and deceit, light penetrates.
Presented as chaste virgins unto Christ, we submit our souls.
No longer weighed down by worldly concerns, the weight lifts.
As potency and virtue take hold, we become invincible in Him.

Adding moral excellence to our faith, His goodness releases.
As His goodness releases, many are led into repentance.
As hearts fill with hope and expectation, His glory descends.
As vessels of salt spread, His purity begins to wash away filth.
As living stones joined together in unity, the bulwark strengthens.

With the Chief Cornerstone in place, He builds us together.
Coming to Him as lively stones, He places strategically.
As the building is fitted and framed together, His glory fills.
Growing into a holy temple, it stands firmly against the tide.
No longer contaminated by the world, we give all glory to Him.

Prayer

Father God, help me remain pure amid all of the debaucheries taking place in the world.

~

May the blessing of God, the Father, be upon you mightily as you resist the cultural norms that are attempting to squeeze the life of God out of you. May you hold tight to the paths of righteousness.

Day 30

Transformed by God's Word and Spirit

God has given two great sources to help us in our Christian journey—His word and Spirit. Our path in life is a life-long journey of being transformed into the image of Christ from glory to glory. With the help of His word and Spirit at our disposal, the journey is made possible. We experience this transformation or the sanctification process in every aspect of our lives. This process happens by washing water through God's word[109] and our relationship with the Holy Spirit.

As born-again Christians, our lives should constantly go through a transformation from glory to glory. We have two agents working with us to help us in this transformation process — God's Holy Word and the Holy Spirit.

Psalm 19:7-9 *The law of the Lord is perfect, converting the soul; the testimony of the Lord is sure, making wise the simple;* ⁸ *the statutes of the Lord are right, rejoicing the heart; the commandment of the Lord is pure, enlightening the eyes;* ⁹ *the fear of the Lord is clean, enduring forever; the judgments of the Lord are true and righteous altogether.*

The above is an enlightening passage of Scripture that reveals the transforming power of God's word. As the writer of the book of Hebrews says, *"The word of God is living and powerful, and sharper than any two-edged sword, piercing even the division of soul and spirit, and of joints and marrow, and is a discerner of thoughts and intents of the heart."*[110]

2 Corinthians 3:17-18 *Now the Lord is the Spirit, and where the Spirit of the Lord is, there is liberty.* ¹⁸ *But we all with unveiled faith, beholding as in a mirror, the*

---

[109] Ephesians 5:26
[110] Hebrews 4:12

The Rise of the Anointed Ones – Transformed by God's Word and Spirit

glory of the Lord, are being transformed into the same image from glory to glory, just as by the Spirit of the Lord.

As seen from the above passages of Scripture, the word of God and the Holy Spirit have the power to transform our lives from glory to glory into the image of Christ as they work together. God gave us His divine nature to accomplish all that God desires to do in and through us. We have the mind of Christ. As we fully embrace the life-changing principles in God's word and freely submit to the work of the Holy Spirit, this transformation process activates in our lives. His Word can convert our souls as His Holy Spirit brings us into the beautiful liberty we have in Christ.

> As we embrace the power of the Holy Spirit working in conjunction with His Word, He fills our minds with wisdom and revelation transforming our thinking into the way God thinks.

The testimony of God's word is sure. We can stake our lives on it. As His Word says, *"The words of the Lord are pure words, like silver tried in a furnace of earth, purified seven times."*[111] As we purpose to trust in the divine inspiration of God's word and believe in our hearts that it is true, His word becomes a reality in our lives and begins the conversion process of our souls, transforming us into Christ's likeness.

As we embrace the power of His Holy Spirit working in conjunction with His Word, He not only begins to burn the chaff in our lives,[112] but fills our minds with wisdom and revelation, transforming our thinking into the way God thinks. The mind of Christ becomes a part of who we are in Him, giving us the same power that was in the life of Jesus Christ.[113] God transforms us from carnal thinking humans to spiritually-minded men and women of God. His power works mightily in us, making us more than conquerors in all of life's situations. This transformation process should be taking place in every born-again Christian. Paul expresses this thought exquisitely to the church at Ephesus in his letter to them.

Ephesians 1:17-19 *that the God of our Lord Jesus Christ, the Father of glory, may give to you the spirit of wisdom and revelation in the knowledge of Him, ¹⁸ the eyes of your understanding being enlightened; that you may know what is the hope of His calling, what are the riches of the glory of His inheritance in*

---

[111] Psalm 12:6
[112] Matthew 3:11-12
[113] Romans 8:11

the saints, [19] and what is the exceeding greatness of His power toward us who believe, according to the working of His mighty power.

No matter who we are, God's thoughts and ways, through His Spirit and Word, can make us wise in Him. If we desire to be wise in the ways of God, our Father, we must humble ourselves as little children to be fully converted.[114] As we fully embrace His thoughts and methods, which are much higher than ours, we become like Him. If we disagree with Him, we say that our thinking is better than His. Whether in ignorance or rebellion, this is either foolish or blatant pride that has the potential of making us stumble and not inherit the blessings He has in store for us. His judgments are pure and righteous in everything. As we freely submit to Him every area of our thought processes, we bring our thoughts into His captivity, which has the power to convert our souls and tear down the strongholds of wrong thinking.[115] As a man thinks in his heart, so is he.

Poem: Transformation through Conversion

Crying out to God for mercy, we come looking for truth.
Wise in our own eyes, all that's seen and heard is distorted.
Perfect in all His ways, He calls us to His righteousness.
With the power to convert our souls, He draws to His Word.
Humbling ourselves before Him, we acknowledge His ways.

His thoughts and ways so much higher than ours, He invites.
Offering a kingdom without observation, He introduces.
Offering wisdom and revelation, He's seen, true and righteous.
As His word touches the spirit, passion ignites to explore.
Breathing upon His Word, His Spirit sparks emergence.

His Word purified over and over; we believe and trust.
Giving ourselves to His Word and Spirit, change materializes.
Enlightened by His Spirit, truth settles and sifts thru the spirit.
As impurities flow to the surface, the heart rejoices in truth.
With the hope of His calling imparted, His power is tested.

As divine inspiration imparts, the mind of Christ transforms.
Transforming our thoughts, old ways of thinking disintegrate.
Making wise the simple, we come forth enlightened in His ways.
Choosing to walk according to His ways, He works mightily.

---

[114] Matthew 18:3-4
[115] 2 Corinthians 10:4-6

The Rise of the Anointed Ones – Transformed by God's Word and Spirit

Filled with His divine nature, His fruit explodes bringing honor.

Transformed into His likeness, conversion becomes our reality.
From glory to glory, staring into His image, we are changed.
With the eyes of our understanding wide open, we experience.
As His greatness takes root, we rejoice in all that's imparted.
Knowing when we see Him, we shall be like Him, faith explodes.

Prayer

Heavenly Father, help me submit to Your authority through Your word and Spirit freely. Allow Your Word to transform my thoughts to align with Your ways and thoughts. Fill my mind with fresh revelation and wisdom as I rely on the Holy Spirit to lead and guide me throughout the day.

~

May the blessings of God the Father be on your life as you fully embrace His righteousness in every aspect of your life. May His ways rejoice in your heart as you cling to Him in godly fear.

Day 31

Swimming Against the Current

If you have ever swum upstream in a stream or a river, you quickly realized it took more effort. As Christians, we must understand that the worldly current we find ourselves in is a fast-flowing stream. Jesus called us to swim against the current of the world. If our faith is weak, we may find ourselves drowning in unbelief. We must make every effort to build faith muscles to survive in this ungodly climate. Survival and overcoming the cunning ways of the enemy will depend upon seeking those things above rather than earthly things.

Colossians 3:1-3 If then you were raised with Christ, seek those things which are above, where Christ is, sitting at the right hand of God. ² Set your mind on things above, not on things on the earth, ³ For you died, and your life is hidden with Christ in God.

Because we are sensual beings, it is more natural to allow our minds to flow towards all that is earthly. As born-again Christians, Paul encourages us to resist the earthly realm by setting or fixing our senses and affections on the eternal weight of glory rather than our momentary afflictions.[116] Understanding that our time in this life is just a vapor compared to the eternal weight of glory, we must be spiritually minded rather than carnally minded.

Romans 8:5-6 For those who live according to the flesh set their minds on the things of the flesh, but those who live according to the Spirit, the things of the Spirit. ⁶ For to be spiritually minded is life and peace.

---

[116] 2 Corinthians 4:16-18

The Rise of the Anointed Ones – Swimming Against the Current

To set our minds on the Spirit and the eternal realm involves a concerted effort on our part. It's something we must press into if we want to receive the rewards of a life governed by the eternal weight of glory rather than momentarily earthly pleasures and pursuits. It doesn't just happen! Because the worldly current is powerful, we must exert effort. What happens when you try to float or do not put much effort when swimming upstream? You find yourself moving downstream even though your motion is moving upstream. The current is more potent than your efforts. Because the worldly stream is so strong, it's hard to tell the difference between believers and unbelievers in today's watered-down versions of Christianity—too many get caught in the current of the world. Paul's vision of eternity caused Him to go against the world's current. Once he received a glimpse of eternity, His confession was, *"To this end I also labor, striving according to His working which works in me mightily."*[117]

> Paul's vision of eternity caused Him to go against the world's current. Once he received a glimpse of eternity, His confession was, *"To this end I also labor, striving according to His working which works in me mightily.*

The world has conditioned us to hope in pleasures that do not satisfy. Yet, God offers a life path wherein we will experience the true pleasures and the fullness of joy found in Him.[118] These are pleasures that not only last a lifetime but throughout eternity as well. Why waste time with the empty pleasures of the world when you can have the true riches and happiness from God who has your best interest at heart? If we truly desire a life of peace and the abundant life Jesus promised, we must set our affections on that which is above. In doing so, we discover Christ is there to give us the strength to swim against the world's current and all that is earthly. We find out, in the process, the Holy Spirit is our divine enabler and helper as we learn to strive according to His working, which works in us mightily.

As we set our affections on the eternal joys and pleasures with Christ as our sufficiency, we can live and move effortlessly against the currents of the world. No longer held back, we fulfill our purpose and destiny to which the Father birthed in us. It was for the joy that was set before Him that Jesus endured the shame of the cross.[119] As we allow this same joy to fill

---

[117] Colossians 1:29
[118] Psalm 16:11
[119] Hebrews 12:1-2

our hearts and minds, God enables us to run with endurance the race He sets before us.

2 Corinthians 4:16-18 Therefore, we do not lose heart. Even though our outward man is perishing, yet the inward man is being renewed day by day. [17] For our light affliction, which is but for a moment, is working for us a far more exceeding and eternal weight of glory, [18] while we do not look at the things which are seen, but at the things which are not seen. For the things which are seen are temporary, but the things which are not seen are eternal."."

Poem: The Eternal Weight of Glory

Caught in a vicious current, struggling to be free, we gain to lose.
Conditioned to place hope in all that doesn't satisfy, we struggle.
Allowing our hearts to flow towards what's earthly, we grapple.
Setting our sights on the eternal, He gives a better way to choose.
With the eternal weight of glory in sight, we strive accordingly.

Pressing hard into all that's been promised, we stroke to gain.
No longer caught in currents spinning, we stroke effortlessly.
As streams of living water flow, we give ourselves to the power.
With His power working in us mightily, we strive accordingly.
No longer slipping backward, with each stroke, forward, we thrust.

Knowing that life is but a vapor that passes quickly, we bow.
With glimpses of eternity shown, hope renewed, faith arises.
A better way revealed the earthly gives way to the eternal.
With pleasures forever, the eternal weight outweighs.
In our wake, worldly pleasures and pursuits, His glory reveals.

With the eternal weight of glory within reach, we press to obtain.
Knowing He's preparing eternal homes, our imaginations run wild.
Knowing there's nothing but eternal beauty and rest, we give praise.
Knowing heaven is pain-free, with no sadness nor crying, we rejoice.
Considering the eternal weight of glory, light affliction is now bearable.

Prayer

As I open my heart to You today, asking for faith to resist the currents of the world, empower me through the Holy Spirit to work Your eternal weight of glory to move against the currents of worldly pleasures and thinking effortlessly.

~

The Rise of the Anointed Ones – Swimming Against the Current

May the blessing of God be with you today as you set your heart and mind on all that God has for you in this life and the one to come.

Day 32

Concerns That Dominate

We all have a tendency to get bogged down by life-dominating concerns, to the extent, we do not have the energy or the time to give ourselves to God's purposes. When this happens it's hard to see past our problems into the wonderful life Jesus promised that takes care of our worldly concerns. Consumed with humanly concerns, we may tend to blind ourselves to spiritual realities. Let us not be stumbling blocks to all that God has in store for us during this critical time of our world's history, lest Jesus rebukes us as He did with Peter.

Matthew 16:23 *(NIV) Jesus turned and said to Peter, "Get behind me, Satan! You are a stumbling block to me;* ***you do not have in mind the concerns of God, but merely human concerns.***"

As Jesus said to Peter, *"You do not have in mind the concerns of God, but merely human concerns,"* the same could be said about most of us if we are honest with ourselves. Are we more concerned about all of our humanly concerns than what's on the heart of our Heavenly Father, God?

What are the situations that dominate our lives? Let's face it, in this life; we have many concerns. The most common problems we all deal with are finances, health, relationships, working environment, career pressures, boredom, confusion, safety, security, and more. Which of these concerns dominate your daily thinking versus what God's will and purposes are? This is something we should ask ourselves on a daily basis.

As James, the Lord's brother, said, *"You don't know what will happen tomorrow. For what is your life? It is even a vapor that appears for a little time and then vanishes away. Instead, you ought to say, 'If the Lord wills, we shall do this and that.'"*[120]

---

[120] James 4:14-15

The Rise of the Anointed Ones – Concerns that Dominate

Our world today is imploding right before our very eyes. If we're not careful, we could get caught up in the chaos and the instability of our times. We could become more concerned about our security, safety, and well-being by becoming distracted from that which is on the Father's heart. Do we want to become stumbling blocks to all that the Father wants to do in and through us? Rather than giving in to humanly concerns, should we not yoke ourselves to Him in all that He's doing in this season? Who or what we are yoking ourselves to is a question we must answer if we are to be salt and light amid the chaos! As His anointed ones, we are to arise amid the chaos.

> If we're not careful, we could get caught up in the chaos and the instability of our times. We could become more concerned about our security, safety, and well-being by becoming distracted from that which is on the Father's heart.

After rebuking Peter for his carnal thinking, Jesus' response to Peter and the other disciples was to take up their crosses and follow Him. As we take up our cross daily and put our trust entirely in God, we are free from worldly concerns.

Matthew 16:24 *Jesus said to his disciples, "Whoever wants to be my disciple must deny themselves and take up their cross and follow me. [25] For whoever wants to save their life will lose it, but whoever loses their life for me will find it.*

In Matthew's gospel, Jesus deals with the issue of how we should handle the concerns of life. He says we shouldn't worry about what we eat, drink, wear, or even where to invest. His answer was to seek the kingdom of God and His righteousness. He said that all these things would be added to us when we do.[121] In other words, we are to be more concerned with God's concerns rather than merely human concerns. If we want to save our lives during chaos, we must wholeheartedly take up His cross and follow Him.

Matthew 6:33-34 *But seek first the kingdom of God and His righteousness, and all these things will be added unto you. [34] Therefore do not worry about tomorrow, for tomorrow will worry about its own things. Sufficient for the day is its own trouble.*

In Luke's gospel, we find the story of Jesus visiting the home of two sisters: Mary and Martha. As Jesus taught, Mary was sitting at the feet of Jesus, hanging onto every word coming out of His mouth, while her sister was busing herself serving those in attendance. Martha finally got so perturbed that Mary wasn't helping she tried to coax Jesus into making her

---

[121] Matthew 6:19-21

The Rise of the Anointed Ones – Concerns that Dominate

help. She came to Jesus and said, *"Lord, do you not care that my sister has left me to serve alone? Therefore, tell her to help me."* Jesus' reply to her was, *"Martha, Martha, you are worried and troubled about many things. But one thing is needed, and Mary has chosen the good part, which will not be taken from her."*[122]

How many of us are more like Martha than Mary? We are so concerned with worrying about the many things that encompass our lives; we don't have time to sit with Jesus and hear how He can make our lives better by casting all our care and concerns upon Him. Jesus' words to us are, *"Come unto me, all you who labor and are heavy laden, and I will give you rest. Take my yoke upon you and learn from Me, for I am gentle and lowly in heart, and you will find rest for your souls. For my yoke is easy, and my burden is light."*[123] Even though the cross may seem heavy to pick up and bear, His promise to us is, His yoke is easy, and His burden is light.

Rather than being a stumbling block to a world immersed in chaos, let us purpose to be salt and light to those in our fields of harvest. Let them see the hope that's in us as we cast all our cares and concerns on Him, who delights in making our burdens light. Let us be like Mary and choose the good part. As we draw close to God in intimacy, His concerns become our concerns.

Poem: Concerns that Dominate

In a world dominated by human concerns, we struggle.
Concerned about life's issues, in chaos, we crumble.
Immersed in the surrounding chaos, we gain to lose.
Our minds filled with anxiety and worry; we confuse.
Struggling to be free, we question thoughts that trouble.

Problems intensifying as life implodes, we look for direction.
Looking to the heavens above, we ask and seek for answers.
From within, a gentle voice whispers amidst the chaos.
Hearing, "Turning our hearts toward God's concerns," we listen.
Questioning, the heart begins to ponder the significance.

In humility, without feeling defensive, we listen for wisdom.
Guided by God's word, we look for solutions that dissipate.
Desiring freedom from all concerns that dominate, we search.

---

[122] Luke 10:40-42
[123] Matthew 11:28-30

The Rise of the Anointed Ones – Concerns that Dominate

Looking to the words of Jesus, we discover the cross, once lost.
Lost in the struggle, the cross became a stumbling block.

The cross fully embraced, once denied, new life emerges.
Like Mary, who chose the good part, we sit at His feet.
Filled with peace, new insight fills the mind with hope.
His concerns now ours, His Spirit dominates in chaos.
Embracing His yoke, burdens lifted, He's now in control.

Prayer

Thank you, Lord, that I can cast all my cares on You, rather than being overly concerned with the cares that try to dominate my thinking. Help me be faithful to sit at Your feet and learn how to cast my cares and concerns upon You continually.

~

May God bless you mightily as you go forth into your daily routines yoked together with Christ in all things. May your concerns no longer dominate your life and thinking as you immerse yourselves in the matters of our Heavenly Father.

Day 33

Flames of Fire

The Holy Spirit came to the early disciples with tongues of fire, transforming them into flames of fire as they went forth fulfilling the Father's prophetic purposes. God wants to do the same with us as we believe on His only begotten Son.

The Father's only begotten Son came to give us salvation that brings us into fellowship with the Father, Son, and Holy Spirit. He came to reveal the Father in all His glory by showing us how great salvation is. As Peter mentions in his first epistle, salvation is something the prophets and the angels of God desired to partake of but couldn't.[124] However, God blesses us beyond measure as recipients of all that He has planned and purposed for humankind. As beneficiaries of His great salvation, we have been made flames of fire.

Psalm 104:3-4 *He lays the beams of His upper chambers in the waters, who makes His clouds His chariot, who walks on the wings of the wind, ⁴ who makes His angels spirits, His ministers a flame of fire.*

Jesus came in the fullness of time to fulfill the Father's prophetic purpose. The prophet Isaiah spoke of this when he prophesied a Son would be given, called Wonderful, Counselor, Mighty God, Everlasting God, and Prince of Peace.[125] Because the fullness of the Godhead rested upon Him, the Father gave His son names to represent His fullness. It was God in His zeal and sovereignty that brought forth the fulfillment of Isaiah's remarkable prophecy. For every prophetic purpose, His Holy prophets have spoken through the ages; God continues to fulfill in His zeal using His ministers as flames of fire. [126]

Before Jesus can return to earth to set up His throne as it is in Heaven, God must fulfill everything spoken by His holy prophets with the restoration of

---

[124] 1 Peter 1:10-12
[125] Isaiah 9:6-7
[126] 1 Peter 1:10-12, Isaiah 9:6-7, Acts 10:1-16, 2:1-4, , Acts 5:19-20, 12-5-9, Joel 2:28-29, Rev.19:6.

The Rise of the Anointed Ones – Flames of Fire

all things being complete. Peter spoke about this in his message after the healing of the lame man at Solomon's Portico.

Acts 3:19 *"Repent therefore and be converted, that your sins may be blotted out, so that times of refreshing may come from the presence of the Lord, [20] and that He may send Jesus Christ who was preached to you before, [21] whom heaven must receive (retain) until the times of restoration of all things, which God had spoken by the mouth of His Holy prophets since the world began."*

Peter and the others were baptized with the Holy Spirit and fire on the day God fully fulfilled the Feast of Pentecost just as God fulfilled the Feast of Passover by Jesus, the perfect Lamb of God. Then, filled with the power of the Holy Spirit, these disciples went forth like flames of fire just as the prophet Joel prophesied, fulfilling the prophetic purposes of God for their generation. The opening passage on the previous page explains how God brings His prophetic purposes to pass in His sovereignty. He makes His angels spirits and His ministers flames of fire.

> God is preparing His vessels of honor, who will go forth like flames of fire with their passion ignited to fulfill all that His Holy prophets have prophesied concerning the end of the age.

We find this to be true as we study the lives of these early disciples and apostles of Christ throughout the New Testament. When it came time to fulfill the prophecy of Joel, God sent a mighty rushing wind to baptize them in the Holy Spirit. The Holy Spirit came to them with tongues of fire, transforming them into flames of fire as they went forth fulfilling the Father's prophetic purposes.

When it came time to fulfill the prophecies of the Gentiles coming into this great salvation, God orchestrated the event by giving a Gentile non-believer, Cornelius, and a Jewish believer, Peter, visions that brought them together to fulfill this prophetic purpose. As flames of fire, both Cornelius and Peter had to be obedient to the visions they had received. But it was God in His zeal that made it happen. The example of Cornelius and Peter is a beautiful picture of how God's sovereignty and our free meet together to fulfill prophetic purposes. We also see how God used angels to bring forth His prophetic purposes in both the lives of Peter and Paul.

As we approach the end of the age, there are many prophetic purposes God must yet fulfill with His flames of fire before He releases Jesus from Heaven. God is preparing His vessels of honor, who will go forth like flames of fire with their passion ignited to fulfill all that His Holy prophets have prophesied concerning the end of the age.

Will you be a prepared vessel with the proper amount of oil in your lamp to be ignited, or will you be found sleeping when the Holy Spirit comes upon us like a mighty rushing wind as He did with the early disciples? The choice is ours to make. Now is the time for His bride to make herself ready. When God decides to move suddenly, it comes without notice.

Poem: Wings of the Wind, Flames of Fire

He comes on the wings of the wind, filling our vessels.
With clouds as His chariot, He comes setting us aflame.
With rushing winds, He comes with tongues of fire to ignite.
Filled with flaming fire, His vessels go forth in His Name.
With great expectancy, His name is proclaimed with might.

With passion ignited, transforming power produces purity.
As the chaff begins to burn, the old disappears into ashes.
As a gentle breeze blows, newness comes with surety.
With each new day, there's an expectation of what's ahead.
As the chaff continues to burn, old strongholds disintegrate.

Made anew by His Spirit, vision, and purpose awaken.
With divine abilities, gifts birthed, He gives sail to the wind.
Flames igniting with explosive power, He gives birth to ministry.
With the mind of Christ, confidence explodes with desire.
Clothed with splendor, He makes His ministers flames of fire.

From wings of the wind, breathing on dry bones, they awaken.
As the Lord performs in His zeal, He fulfills what's written.
As flames of fire, His Church the Bride ministers to fulfill.
With explosive power, He infuses with authority on high.
With mighty winds, He gives sail to those standing by.

Fully clothed in her fullness, the Bride stands fully dressed.
A chaste virgin, measured in His stature, she radiates His fullness.
Wedding garments placed, she's made ready for her day, now near.
From the clouds of heaven, the Bridegroom comes to receive her.
Joined together, she's known as He's known, now consummated.

Prayer

Heavenly Father, I commit my heart to you. Make me one of Your ministers going forth as a flame of fire, fulfilling Your prophetic purposes.

~

May the blessing of the Lord be with you as you sanctify and consecrate yourself. Then, filling you with the explosive power of the Holy Spirit, may you go forth fulfilling His prophetic purposes for this generation.

Day 34

The Joyful Sound of God's Spirit

One of the most extraordinary sounds we have the privilege of hearing is the joyful sound of God's Spirit. When God speaks, whether a gentle whisper or revelation of how He works in our lives, a sense of joy floods our soul.

Psalm 89:15-16 *Blessed are the people who know the joyful sound! They walk, O Lord, in the light of your countenance.* ^{16} *In Your Name they rejoice all day long, and in your countenance, they are exalted all day long, and in Your righteousness, they are exalted.*

For most of us, when we accepted Christ as our Lord and Savior, we had a sense of pure joy that flooded our souls. Our spirits were able to hear the joyful sound that emanated from the throne of God as it brought us into His presence. We were counted among those who could experience what this joyful sound revealed to us about our Father and the Lord Jesus Christ. With the realization that He completely forgave us of our sins along with our guilt and shame, we experienced the fullness of joy that came from hearing and responding to the joyful sound. Strengthened by joy with the removal of condemnation, we rejoiced in all that Jesus accomplished when He embraced the cross and grave. With the joyful sound flooding our souls, we came into an understanding that we were made righteous by the blood of Christ. [127]

Because of what Christ accomplished for us, we can continually come boldly into the His presence without fear or intimidation. The Father gave us the ability to stand in the perfect righteousness of Jesus rather than our own, which He deemed as filthy rags. As we exalt in His righteousness

---

[127] 2 Corinthians 5:21

The Rise of the Anointed Ones – The Joyful Sound of God's Spirit

rather than hanging our heads in shame and defeat through our righteousness, He blesses beyond belief. How can we help but continually hear the joyful sound emanating from the heavens above as the angels rejoice over us while we bask in His great love?

The problem is we have an enemy who does not want us to hear the joyful sound of God's Spirit as it penetrates our hearts day after day. Satan knows the joy of the Lord is our strength and will do whatever he can to keep us from hearing it as it touches our spirits. Therefore, touched by His grace, we now yield to the Holy Spirit daily so that His joy continually resounds in our hearts on a daily basis.

As we continually draw from the wells of salvation and fellowship with the Holy Spirit, we experience the living water Jesus spoke of when He said, *"If anyone thirsts, let him come to me and drink."* He then went on to say, *"He who believes in Me, as the Scripture has said, out of your heart will flow rivers of living water."*[128] When Jesus spoke these words, He was referring to our relationship with the Holy Spirit, which allows us to continually hear the joyful sound that emanates from the throne of God. As we draw living water from the wells of salvation, He fills us with the fullness the Holy Spirit desires to impart into our lives.

> Our relationship with the Holy Spirit allows us to continually hear the joyful sound that emanates from the throne of God.

Isaiah 13:2-3 *"Behold God is my salvation. I will trust and not be afraid; for 'YAH, the LORD is my strength and song; He also has become my salvation.'"* [3] *Therefore, with joy, you will draw water from the wells of salvation.*

The wells of salvation contain all the benefits of this great salvation that enrich our souls and refresh us daily. We continually receive forgiveness, healing, redemption from destruction, tender mercies, good things, daily renewal, and more from His wells.[129] The caveat is we must put forth the effort to draw from His wells by calling upon the Lord and putting our trust in His sufficiency, even when things don't seem to be going our way. As we wait on Him and stay on the path of righteousness, He continually fills our hearts and minds with peace, love, joy, and His righteousness.[130] Our Father in Heaven desires to fill our hearts with wisdom and revelation in the knowledge of Him as we trust in Him for all things.

---

[128] John 7:37-39
[129] Psalm 103:1-5
[130] Romans 14:17

Poem: The Joyful Sound

Awakened by a sound emanating from God's throne, we listen.
With hearts beating fast in anticipation, joy floods with vision.
In wonderment, we stand amazed as joy penetrates the soul.
Drawn to Him, intense joy flooding the senses, we discover.
Giving ourselves, His sound reverberates with cleansing power.

As sins wash away, guilt and shame disappear into the night.
Strengthened by the joyful sound, in His benefits, we delight.
As tender mercies take hold, angels above rejoice over us.
No longer bound by sin and darkness, we delight in salvation.
Redeemed from destructive ways, the joyful sound plays on.

Knowing the joyful sound strengthens, Satan comes to steal.
With traps and snares, he comes to deceive and beguile.
In truth, not ignorant of his devices, we stand ready to defend.
As he hurls his darts, taking the shield of faith, we contend.
Filled with joy, in the light of His countenance, we give praise.

From the wells of salvation, we continually draw as joy fills.
Filled with the spirit of wisdom and revelation, His joy fulfills.
Called according to His purposes, His joyful sound leads.
Immersed into His Spirit, with wisdom, revelation accedes.
Filled with anticipation for things to come, joy exceeds.

Prayer

Thank you, Lord, for giving me the wells of salvation. Help me, never take the benefits You have poured into my life for granted. May The joyful sound of Your Spirit continually emanate from me in all that You've called me to be and do.

~

May your heart be continually filled with the joyful sound of God's Spirit as you give yourself wholeheartedly to all that He's called us to.

Day 35

Beware of the Antichrist Spirit

As followers of Jesus, we know sooner or later the Antichrist will arrive on the scene. He will come as the son of perdition, opposing and exalting himself above all that is called God. He will sit among the world and God's people showing himself as God. Rather than focusing on who the antichrist is or his coming, we should be more concerned with the antichrist spirit, which is already alive and well among us, just as it was in the early Church.[131]

I John 2:18-19 Little children, it is the last hour; and as you have heard that the Antichrist is coming, even now many antichrists have come, by which we know that it is the last hour. ¹⁹ They went out from us, but they were not of us; for if they had been of us, they would have continued with us; but they went out that they might be made manifest, that none of them were of us.

Jesus warned us that many false teachers and prophets would come to deceive God's people before His second coming.[132] Paul warned us about listening to those who preach a different Jesus or gospel than what he preached.[133] Unfortunately, the truth of the matter is that these false apostles, prophets, teachers, pastors, and evangelists are already amongst us, filling our pulpits with lies and half-truths born out of the antichrist spirit that is alive and well in today's Church world.

Those in positions of authority who have been taken captive by the antichrist spirit are in error. They unwittingly draw God's people away from solid biblical teaching designed to produce God's purpose and fruit of the Spirit in their lives. It is essential to understand that most of them

---

[131] 2 Thessalonians 2:3-4
[132] Matthew 24:11
[133] 2 Corinthians 11:4, Galatians 1:6-9

The Rise of the Anointed Ones – Beware of the Antichrist Spirit

are unaware they have been taken captive by the antichrist spirit. Satan deceived them by their self-will, which led them into captivity.

When we look at the significant traits that caused Lucifer to fall from his exalted position in the heavens, we discover it was self-will. The attributes in the antichrist spirit and the Antichrist are the same ones that caused Satan's expulsion from the third realm of heaven. At one point, Satan was the most beautiful of all the archangels. Unfortunately, he became filled with self-will and pride and wanted to be like God.

The Antichrist will be the incarnation of Satan, just as Jesus was the incarnation of God, the Father. Just as Lucifer tried to exalt himself above God, so it is with the man of sin. The prophets: Ezekiel and Isaiah, expose Satan's true colors in the following passages.

> The antichrist spirit has its way when we fail to embrace the cross's message and repentance. A gospel that doesn't include repentance and fully embraces what it means to pick up your cross and follow Jesus is what Paul called "another gospel" and warned us to avoid.

Ezekiel 28:13-15 You were in Eden, the garden of God; every precious stone was your covering: the sardius, topaz, and diamond, beryl, onyx, and jasper, sapphire, turquoise, and emerald with gold. The workmanship of your timbrels and pipes was prepared for you on the day you were created. ^{14} *"You were the anointed cherub who covers; I established you; you were on the holy mountain of God; you walked back and forth in the midst of fiery stones.* ^{15} *You were perfect in your ways from the day you were created, till iniquity was found in you.*

Before his fall, Satan was one of the most influential angelic beings in the universe, being of great beauty. His name was Lucifer. He held a high position in heaven before he became Satan. He was perfect in every way but abused his position and beauty, which brought destruction upon himself and the angels who followed him.

In the preceding passage and the one below, we see descriptions of Lucifer's beauty and abilities and the characteristics that caused him to lose his anointed position. The character traits found in Lucifer are similar to what Paul mentions to the Thessalonians about the man of sin and perdition, the Antichrist.[134]

Isaiah 14:13-14 For you have said in your heart: I will ascend into heaven, I will exalt my throne above the stars of God; I will also sit on the mount of the

---

[134] 2 Thessalonians 2:3-4

The Rise of the Anointed Ones – Beware of the Antichrist Spirit

congregation on the farthest sides of the north; ¹⁴ I will ascend above the heights of the clouds, I will be like the Most High.

Notice all the "I will's" of Satan. He was inundated with self-will. Lucifer wanted to sit as God and wanted his throne to be in heaven, not on earth. The name "Most High" in the Bible is the word *"El Elohim,"* not only means "Most High," but also means "the possessor of heaven and earth." Lucifer attempted a rebellious mutiny, with a third of the angels following him without realizing how mighty God was. His final attempt at his rebellious uprising will be when he transforms himself into the Antichrist.

2 Timothy 2:3-4 *Let no one deceive you by any means; for that Day will not come unless the falling away comes first, and the man of sin is revealed, the son of perdition, ⁴ who opposes and exalts himself above all that is called God or that is worshiped, so that he sits as God in the temple of God, showing himself that he is God.*

Unfortunately, many present-day church cultures are defrauded by Satan's deceptive tactics. As a result, church cultures exist that don't properly acknowledge the Lordship of Jesus Christ. The antichrist spirit has its way when we fail to embrace the cross's message and repentance. A gospel that doesn't include repentance and fully embraces what it means to pick up your cross and follow Jesus is what Paul called "another gospel" and warned us to avoid. A false gospel message produces self-willed Christians susceptible to the antichrist spirit. Jesus warned us about how important it is to take up our cross and follow Him wholeheartedly.

Matthew 10:38 *And he who does not take his cross and follow after Me is not worthy of me.*

Caught up in self-will, those who do not fully embrace the cross of Christ will be easily persuaded by the antichrist spirit. The problem of self-will is paramount with those in leadership, which is why Paul encouraged Timothy not to ordain elders who were self-willed. The intended purpose of the cross is to destroy our self-will in the same way it did for Jesus when He said, *"Not my will, but Your will be done."* When we say yes to Jesus and take up our cross to follow Him, we are saying, *"Not my will, but Your will be done,"* in the same manner that He did. We are to emulate Jesus in all things, becoming like-minded or having the same attitude.

Philippians 2:5-8 *Let this mind (attitude NASB) be in you, which was also in Christ Jesus, ⁶ who, being in the form of God, did not consider it robbery to be equal with God, ⁷ but made Himself of no reputation, taking the form of a bondservant, and coming in the likeness of men. ⁸ And being found in appearance* *as a man, He humbled Himself and became obedient to the point of death, even the death of the cross.*

Thankfully, God has given us a way to destroy the self-will within us. We all have it, whether we admit it or not. It's a part of our sinful nature that must be destroyed or crucified with Christ. To be among those who rise as the anointed ones in Christ's fullness during the final harvest yet to come, we must submit to the Father of spirits. In doing so, our self-will is destroyed.

Hebrews 12:9 *Furthermore, we have human fathers who corrected us, and we paid them respect. Shall we not much more readily be in subjection to the Father of spirits and live.*

To relieve ourselves of self-will not only involves submitting to our Heavenly Father but also one to another. We are not to be a law unto ourselves. We must be in relationship with the members of the body of Christ God has placed us in. When we submit to one another, it helps us stay accountable for our actions and remain humble and obedient. Once self-will is destroyed, other fleshly and sinful areas are much easier to destroy as well.

Galatians 2:20 *I have been crucified with Christ; it is no longer I who live, but Christ lives in me; and the life I now live in the flesh I live by faith in the Son of God, who loved me and gave Himself for me.*

Let us continually be aware and on guard towards the antichrist spirit that wants to invade our ranks and steal from us what the Holy Spirit has poured into our lives.

Poem: The Beast from the Sea

As the beast from the sea, the man of sin comes scheming.
Horns and crowns on his head, he comes blaspheming.
Like a leopard and feet of a bear, he comes with vengeance.
A mouth like a lion, he receives power to kill and devour.
With great authority, he's released with Satan's full power.

With hate and deception, he comes to destroy and terminate.
In the complete incarnation of evil, he comes to impersonate.
Coming as the man of sin, he sits as God in the temple.
Opposing, above all that is called God, he exalts himself.
With rage, war breaks out in heaven, causing all to tremble.

Cast down from heaven, he wages war against all Christians.
Coming to kill, he strikes those who are to rule the kingdom.

The Rise of the Anointed Ones – Beware of the Antichrist Spirit

Caught up as first fruits, they escape as God takes possession.
With rage, Satan sends a flood to drown and destroy the Bride.
Rescued on the wings of a great eagle, the Father gives ride.

Given power over the remnant left behind, he seeks to destroy.
With strong delusion he comes, given exceeding power to trap.
With signs and wonders, he deceives those on earth with ploys.
With great power, he causes all to receive his mark or be killed.
As his mark is received, multitudes fall away, being deceived.

With the righteous ones removed, the fury of the Lord is released.
To those who receive his mark, seven angels appear with plagues.
With grievous sores, scorching fire, and earthquakes, He releases.
Kept from the hour of trial upon the whole world, the Bride escapes.
For three and a half years, they're tormented while the Bride feasts.

Taking vengeance with 10,000's of His saints, Jesus descends.
Those killed by the beast rise to meet Him as they ascend.
From her refuge, the Bride rises to meet them in the air.
Bound for a thousand years, the beast no longer blasphemes or snares.
Tormented day and night, they're cast into the fiery lake with the tares.

Prayer

Thank you, Lord, for giving imparting Your Holy Spirit into my life. I freely submit unto You and give You my life so that I will be free of the self-will that hinders me from time to time. Help me be faithful to embrace the cross so that my self-will is destroyed daily.

~

May you be one of God's anointed ones who resists all that the antichrist spirit represents in this world.

Day 36

Exhibiting Moral Excellence

Today's world is highly contaminated by the sinfulness and rebellion spewing out of the mouths of those who are under the sway of the evil one, Satan. We live in a perverse generation of which Satan is working hard to infiltrate every sphere of our cultures with his venom. As Peter wrote, we need to be saved from a perverse generation.

Acts 2:40 And with many other words, he testified and exhorted them, saying, "Be saved from this perverse generation."

Our generation has become just as perverse as the one Peter spoke of in the Scripture above. Unfortunately, God's people are also getting swallowed up by Satan's lies and treachery. We must heed the call to be saved from this perverse generation as Peter encourages us to, lest we fall into the traps and snares Satan puts in our paths.

We live in a season in which wickedness and a lack of morality are on the increase. While our cultures promote and condone sexual promiscuity, homosexuality, gender preference, abortion, filthy and coarse language, plus much more with a hate-filled mindset, the Church needs to understand the importance of embracing moral excellence. All of which was just mentioned is flaunted flagrantly through social media, music, television, movies, books, magazines, and other media sources. If all of this is not enough, judgment and justice are compromised too. With rioting and looting in our streets without consequences, seeing criminals set free, the corruption of our justice system crumbles as justice is turned back.[135] All of this is happening in our world today because much of the Church has abdicated its authority. It is no longer the pillar of truth. As a result, it has allowed truth to fall in the streets.[136]

---

[135] Isaiah 59:14
[136] Jeremiah 5:30-31

The Rise of the Anointed Ones – Exhibiting Moral Excellence

Ecclesiastes 3:16 *Moreover I saw under the sun: In the place of judgment, wickedness was there; and in the place of righteousness, iniquity was there.*

With our world plagued by murder, abortion, teenage pregnancies, rioting, gang violence, rampant drug usage, and many other cultural ills, it's time for God's people to rise and shine during this season of darkness. If our light is hidden, we may find ourselves giving in to Satan's wiles while abdicating our authority over him and his domains. We must heed the prophet Isaiah's prophecy, which is relevant for these times as darkness begins to cover the earth.

Isaiah 60:1-2 *Arise shine, for your light has come! And the glory of the Lord is risen upon you. ² For behold, the darkness shall cover the earth, and deep darkness the people, but the Lord will arise over you, and His glory will be seen upon you.*

To heed the call, we must commit ourselves to moral excellence. In this desperate hour, the Church needs to exhibit a sense of moral excellence to bring salvation to those who are in desperate need of it before Jesus returns to judge the earth and its inhabitants. As Paul encouraged young Timothy when he said, *"Take heed to yourself and to the doctrine. Continue in them, for in doing this you will save both yourself and those who hear you,"* so it is with us. We are to be examples to believers and unbelievers in word, conduct, love, spirit, faith, and purity.[137]

Peter also issues a strong appeal in his second epistle. He urges us to add certain ingredients to our faith; otherwise, we, too, will fall and be swept away in this tide of wickedness.

2 Peter 1:5-6 *But also for this very reason, giving all diligence, add to your faith virtue, to virtue knowledge, ⁶ to knowledge self-control, to self-control perseverance, to perseverance godliness.*

As Christians, God calls us to stand against the tide of evil and wickedness by adding virtue or moral excellence to our faith. There have been other times throughout the history of our world when sin and violence have invaded the ranks of God's chosen people in significant ways as well. Now is such a time to be saved from a perverse generation. God calls us as Christians to stand in opposition to all we see and hear while walking in a moral excellence that directly contrasts the evil that is rapidly taking over the cultures of the world.

---

[137] 1 Timothy 4:12,16

The Rise of the Anointed Ones – Exhibiting Moral Excellence

People of courage are needed to stand against this tide of wickedness and moral depravity sweeping up against the landscapes of the world. Unless we are committed to moral excellence, we too, shall be swept aside in this tide of sin and evil.

2 Peter 1:10 Therefore, brethren, be even more diligent to make your calling and election sure, for if you do these things, you will never stumble.

Peter says, *"We must add virtue to our faith."* Virtue is defined as moral excellence. Thayer's' Greek Lexicon defines it as a virtuous course of thought, feeling, or action that leads to moral goodness, any particular moral excellence as modesty or purity.

> With our world plagued by murder, teenage pregnancies, rioting, gang violence, rampant drug usage, and many other cultural ills, it's time for God's people to rise and shine during seasons of darkness.

Webster's Dictionary defines virtue as moral excellence, conformity to a standard of right, a particular moral excellence. Manly strength or courage and bravery – An admirable quality or trait; Potency, innocence, especially in women; purity of conduct and intention. Excellence is defined as eminently good: first-class, outstanding. Peter says by the Holy Spirit that God calls us to virtue or moral excellence, of which we must continually add to our faith to keep from being stumbled by the world. The apostle Paul speaks about this as well. He says, concerning moral excellence, we have been espoused to Christ as a chaste virgin.

2 Corinthians 11:2 For I am jealous for you with godly jealousy. For I have betrothed you to one husband, that I may present you as a chaste virgin to Christ.

Thayer's Greek Lexicon defines chaste as pure from carnality, modest, pure from every fault, immaculate. The word virgin means clean, pure, and holy and applies to all Christians who have come to know Jesus Christ as Lord and Savior personally.

1 Peter 1:13-16 Therefore gird up the loins of your mind, be sober, and rest your hope fully upon the grace that is to be brought to you at the revelation of Jesus Christ; [14] as obedient children, not conforming yourselves to the former lusts, as in your ignorance; [15] but as He who called you is holy, you also be holy in all your conduct, [16] because it is written, "Be holy, for I am holy."

As we can see, God desires to have a people striving for moral excellence. Therefore, He expects us to commit to Him in every area of our conduct, such as sexual purity, language, personal integrity, honesty, and the lust of the eyes and flesh.

The Rise of the Anointed Ones – Exhibiting Moral Excellence

Ephesians 5:1-5 *Therefore be followers of God as dear children.* ² *And walk in love, as Christ also has loved us and given Himself for us, an offering, and a sacrifice to God for a sweet-smelling aroma.* ³ **But fornication and all uncleanness or covetousness, let it not even be named among you**, *as is fitting for saints;* ⁴ *neither filthiness, nor foolish talking, nor coarse jesting, which are not fitting, but rather giving of thanks.* ⁵ *For this, you know that no fornicator, unclean person, nor covetous man, who is an idolater, has any inheritance in the kingdom of Christ and God.*

These are all areas in which Christ wants us to add moral excellence to our faith. We should be superior to the world in all of these areas if our light is to shine amid a crooked and perverse generation. Therefore, let us rise as the anointed ones, embracing moral excellence, in every aspect of our lives.

Poem: Awakened from Slumber

In an era of declining morals, gates open wide for immorality.
Reveling in his lustful ways, Satan comes taking advantage.
Caught in the tide of wickedness, God's people become prey.
Like a roaring lion, he comes devouring and exploiting lies.
As truth lies dead in the streets, cultures crumble before our eyes.

God's word tossed aside like pieces of cardboard, sin flourishes.
His word no longer a measurement, His authority diminishes.
With authority undercut, the bulwark of truth gives way to the tide.
As the pillars of truth begin to crumble, Satan is emboldened.
Unleashing his venom, those who oppose are misrepresented.

As Satan's fury unleashes, compromise enters the ranks.
Seeking to be relevant in fear of losing, the Church weakens.
No longer standing strong, authority diminishes as sin creeps in.
Caught in a web of unbelief, the enemy comes, sowing tares.
No longer discernible between wheat and tares, she loses voice.

Asleep in the darkness, she awakens to her condition.
Putting on the armor of light, she begins mending her ways.
Bold as a lion, in His righteousness, she roars with realization.
Standing in the gap, the pillars of truth, she begins to restore.
Embracing the sovereignty of her Lord, she builds with vigor.

Looking sin, squarely in the eyes, a commitment is made.
No longer compromising, she repents, having strayed.
Proclaiming righteousness, she preaches, no longer afraid.

Calling God's people to repent from all sin, she pleads.
Aligned with God's word and sovereignty, she leads.

Identity and morals fully restored; she embraces restoration.
Ready and willing, a workman, unashamed, she strengthens.
Fully submitting to His sovereignty, with Jesus, she co-labors.
With the pillars of truth back in place, His Church, they rebuild.
With gates fully restored, Satan's ploys are quickly quelled.

With the Chief Cornerstone in place, the building is fitly framed.
Embracing the stature of Christ's fullness, evil is no longer inflamed.
Receiving a double portion, they go forth in the power of His Spirit.
As glory fills, multitudes are ushered in before the curtain falls.
Awakened from slumber, they stand fully girded for the final battle.

Prayer

Lord, God, I commit to You and Your authority over my life. Help me to walk in moral excellence in every area. Convict me when You observe me failing in these areas. To those I come in contact with, help me be a shining example of Your moral excellence.

~

May God bless you richly as you respond to the call of moral excellence in all you do and say. May the light of the gospel of Jesus Christ shine on you brightly as you give yourself to moral excellence.

Day 37

God our Stronghold

With the advent of tumultuous times coming upon our world, the potential of getting snared into the ways of the enemy is a threat to all we hold dear. However, God desires us to realize how great a stronghold He is amid whatever adversity we may face in trying times. He is our stronghold during times of trouble, but as the prophet Nahum points out, we must put our complete trust in God for Him to be our stronghold.

Nahum 1:7 The Lord is good, a stronghold in the day of trouble; and He knows those who trust in Him.

God has designed strongholds to provide fortified places of safety for protection during troublous times or when being attacked by demonic forces. They are also positions of strength to be used for offensive attacks. Strongholds were fortified dwellings used as places of protection from the enemy in the Old Testament. We find that David often hid from Saul in wilderness strongholds. The Philistines used them as places to launch their offensive attacks on the nation of Israel, Saul, and his army until Jonathan and his armor-bearer broke through.[138]

1 Samuel 23:14 And David stayed in strongholds in the wilderness and remained in the mountains in the wilderness of Ziph. Saul sought him every day, but God did not deliver him into his hand.

The strongholds David found himself using were physical structures, usually caves high on a mountainside, exceedingly difficult to assault. This imagery in mind inspired writers of the Bible to adapt the word "stronghold" to define powerful, vigorously protected spiritual realities.

A stronghold can be a source of protection from the day of evil when the Lord becomes our stronghold as He did for David. It is also a source of

---

[138] 1 Samuel 14

defense from the influence of the antichrist spirit that is loose in today's world. Unfortunately, our sympathetic thoughts toward evil often defend demonic or sinful activity. Rather than being empathetic, if we want to immerse ourselves in the stronghold of righteousness God desires to encase us in, we must embrace His hatred of sin.

Romans 6:16 *Do you not know that to whom you present yourselves slaves to obey, you are that one's slaves whom you obey. Whether of sin to death or of obedience to righteousness.*

For God to become our stronghold, we must put our complete trust in Him rather than in our ways of thinking and understanding. As we hide in God's thoughts and ways, which are higher than ours, we discover the cave high on His mountainside that protects us from the evil around us. This discovery allows us to tear down the false arguments and every other high thing that exalts itself against the knowledge of God. By bringing every thought into the captivity of Christ rather than leaning on our understanding, we defeat Satan. God knows those who trust in Him. We may fool others with our spiritual games, but it is impossible to fool God, who knows all things. So let us put aside our foolishness and fully submit our hearts to God's way of thinking and make Him our stronghold rather than the false strongholds we build up with our ill devised thinking processes.

> God knows those who trust in Him. We may fool others with our spiritual games, but it is impossible to fool God, who knows all things.

2 Corinthians 10:4-5 *The weapons of our warfare are not carnal but mighty in God for pulling down strongholds, ⁵ casting down arguments and every high thing that exalts itself against the knowledge of God, bringing every thought into captivity to the obedience of Christ.*

As Paul wrote to Timothy concerning the end time climate, we must take heed as we recognize its implications. The days of evil are already upon us. As you can see from the following Scripture, the end time environment Paul spoke of is upon us. This portion of Scripture is a picture of our world today. It will take dwelling in God's stronghold of righteousness not to get swallowed up in this collective mindset that is rampant in today's world.

2 Timothy 3:1-5 *But know this, that in the last days perilous times will come: ² For men will be lovers of themselves, lovers of money, boasters, proud, blasphemers, disobedient to parents, unthankful, unholy, ³ unloving, unforgiving, slanderers, without self-control, brutal, despisers of good, ⁴ traitors, headstrong,*

The Rise of the Anointed Ones – God our Stronghold

haughty, lovers of pleasure rather than lovers of God, [5] having a form of godliness but denying its power. And from such people turn away!

God has equipped us with everything we need to reside within the stronghold He has perfectly designed for who we are in Christ. Because our stronghold in God is a spiritual sphere, it's crucial to understand how the spiritual armor given works to keep us hidden away in His stronghold. He has given us the spiritual armor necessary to protect us from all the sin and wickedness loosed in our world.

Ephesians 6:10-13 *Finally, my brethren, be strong in the Lord and in the power of His might. [11] Put on the whole armor of God, that you may be able to stand against the [a]wiles of the devil. [12] For we do not wrestle against flesh and blood, but against principalities, against powers, against the rulers of the darkness of this age, against spiritual hosts of wickedness in the heavenly places. [13] Therefore take up the whole armor of God, that you may be able to withstand in the evil day, and having done all, to stand.*

The above Scripture reveals the importance of using spiritual armor. May God bless you richly as you give yourselves to discovering your spiritual armor.

Poem: Strongholds of Righteousness

Caught in whirlwinds of unrighteousness, we look for protection.
Filled with sorrow, crying out in agony, we look for direction.
Where to hide, when our world wallows in wickedness, we wonder.
Filled with righteous anger, bordering on rage, we look for relief.
Seeing what destructive sinful mindsets produce, we bow in grief.

Giving ourselves to Him above, we look for peace amid unrest.
Filled with wisdom and revelation, we see beyond all oppressed.
As strongholds of righteousness begin to form, peace settles.
As peace relieves, hope comes alive as the heart rejoices.
With a sense of newness, vision gives birth to new choices.

Looking to Him above with thankful hearts, we place our trust.
As rage gives way to peace, new thoughts emerge that readjust.
With trust reinforced, the stronghold of righteousness protects.
As fiery darts fly, seeking targets, new shields of faith deflect.
No longer wallowing in hopeless fear and trepidation, faith adapts.

With strongholds of righteousness firmly secured, we give praise.
As the enemy advances, we stand ready without fear in His ways.
Taking the kingdom by force, we trample over Satan's attempts.

The Rise of the Anointed Ones – God our Stronghold

To Him, who is greater in us, we stand in the power of His might.
Knowing we have a powerful place of safety; we rest in His fight.

Prayer

Heavenly Father, increase my trust and faith in You. Help me to always rely on Your sufficiency in all that I do. Build a stronghold of protection around me to keep me safe and secure from all of the enemy's attempts to discourage and trap me in his lies.

~

As you give yourself to our Father in Heaven in all things, may you find yourself resting in the divine protection of His stronghold of righteousness.

Day 38

Fortifying our Stronghold with Armor

As born-again Christians, we are thankful for much. One of the most significant aspects of our life in Christ is our spiritual armor. The fundamental way we can show our appreciation is by valuing what God has given us. We do this with our spiritual armor by valuing and using each piece as He intended for the spiritual battles we face. Our stronghold is fortified when we use the weapons of our warfare effectively. We must know how they work in conjunction with the stronghold of righteousness that defines who we are in Christ. With the blood of Christ shed, He keeps us safe from the enemy's devices. Therefore, let's examine each piece of armor He gave us. Some are for defensive purposes, while others are offensive weapons. Both are needed.

Ephesians 6:14-18 Stand therefore, having girded your waist with truth, having put on the breastplate of righteousness, [15] and having shod your feet with the preparation of the gospel of peace; [16] above all, taking the shield of faith with which, you will be able to quench all the fiery darts of the wicked one. [17] And take the helmet of salvation, and the sword of the Spirit, which is the word of God; [18] praying always with all prayer and supplication in the Spirit, being watchful to this end with all perseverance and supplication for all the saints.

God designed each piece of our armor to be a crucial part of the stronghold He established for our safety and well-being. He gave us all the weapons we need, but it is our responsibility to read the instructions found in His word on using them effectively.

The belt of truth is a strong defensive weapon against the lies that spew out of the mouths of Satan and his cohorts that have inundated our cultures. If the truth of God's word is in the recesses of our hearts, we will instantly recognize the lies that appear at our doorsteps. The only way to get His word sown into our hearts is to read, study, and meditate on it. It takes much more than hearing a weekly sermon that is born out of the truth of God's word. In Scripture, we are encouraged to study to show ourselves approved before God as workers without shame. [139] We are also encouraged to be like the Bereans, who searched the Scriptures to ensure what they heard was correct. [140] We are also encouraged to delight and meditate in God's word so that we prosper in all that we do. [141] By giving ourselves to God's word daily, we reinforce God's stronghold of protection around us.

The breastplate of righteousness is essential because we don't stand a chance without it. It has to do with our spiritual understanding of Christ's accomplishments on the cross, where He became our righteousness. [142] He exchanged His righteousness for our sins. One of Satan's effective ploys against us is to accuse and make us feel condemned before God. Because Christ's righteousness now dwells in us, we stand before God without condemnation. The Father only sees us through the perfect righteousness of His Son, Jesus Christ. [143] We have been perfected forever through the one offering made by Christ. As we continue to walk in the Spirit, there is no condemnation to those who are in Christ, Jesus. [144] Therefore, the breastplate of righteousness protects our hearts from all accusations made by Satan. As it says in the book of Hebrews, we have a high priest who sympathizes with our weaknesses, which means we can come boldly to His throne of grace to obtain mercy and help in times of need." [145]

> Our stronghold is fortified when we use the weapons of our warfare effectively. We must know how they work in conjunction with the stronghold of righteousness that defines who we are in Christ.

Our feet shod with the preparation of the Gospel is a necessity if we are to rise as one of His anointed ones. Just as shoes made a Roman soldier, whose custom was to wear sandals as they prepared for battle, Christians must have their feet shod with preparing the gospel of peace. As we share the gospel, we remain in a state of readiness against the enemy. With our

---

[139] 2 Timothy 2:15
[140] Acts 17:10-12
[141] Psalm 1:1-3
[142] 2 Corinthians 5:21
[143] Hebrews 10:14
[144] Romans 8:1
[145] Hebrews 4:15-16

good news shoes on, we stay in a state of high alert, sensitized to the spiritual activity going on around us, whether it is coming from the enemy or hearing the voice of the Holy Spirit. God has called us to be ambassadors of the kingdom regardless of our specific gifts and callings, which entails being ready to give a reason for our hope within.[146] When we are in a state of readiness, the Father reinforces His stronghold of protection around us.

Concerning the shield of faith, Paul says, *"Above all, taking the shield of faith."* Why is the shield of faith so much more important than the other armor pieces? First of all, as the writer of the book of Hebrews reminds us, *"Without faith, it is impossible to please God."*[147] Some of our significant attacks from Satan are doubt, fear, and anxiety. Taking up the shield of faith is our weapon of choice to counter these attacks. The shield of faith is the most vigorous defense we have against attacks from the enemy because it protects the other pieces of armor. As Paul said, *"It can quench all the fiery darts of the wicked one."* It not only protects the other pieces of armor but protects the soldier, from those parts of the soldier that are still unprotected. For instance, the shield protects the breastplate from getting pierced which is a stronghold of righteousness for every area of our lives. We must believe and confess all that we are and have in Christ. As we believe and confess, it builds our faith. As Paul said, *"I believed, and therefore I spoke."*[148] As we determine to take up the shield of faith, believing faith is the substance of things hoped for, the evidence of things not seen, we can quench the fiery darts of wickedness as we dwell in the stronghold of faith.[149]

The helmet of salvation is our next piece of armor. The helmet is an integral part of armor as it protects the only part of our life that the shield of faith can't defend. It represents all that God gave us through our salvation experience. Without the helmet, we would be exposed to the wickedness coming from all of Satan's sources. Thankfully, God has delivered us from Satan's destructive ways. The psalmist makes this clear.

***Psalm 103:2-5** Bless the LORD, O my soul, and forget not all His benefits: ³ Who forgives all your iniquities, Who heals all your diseases, ⁴ Who redeems your life from destruction, Who crowns you with lovingkindness and tender mercies, ⁵ Who*

---

[146] 1 Peter 3:15
[147] Hebrews 11:6
[148] 2 Corinthians 4:13
[149] Hebrews 11:1

satisfies your mouth with good things, So that your youth is renewed like the eagle's.

As we put on the helmet of salvation, all that God gave us in our salvation experience makes us invincible to all of Satan's devices and schemes. We are now ready to take the sword of the Spirit and go forth into battle, knowing greater is He that's within us than he who is in the world as John the beloved disciple writes.

*1 **John 4:4** You are of God little children and have overcome them because He who is in you is greater than he who is in the world.*

The sword of the Spirit is the word of God, which is living and powerful, and sharper than any two-edged sword, piercing even to the division of soul and spirit, and joints and marrow, and is a discerner of the thoughts and intents of the heart.[150] Although the sword of the Spirit is a powerful weapon, it is useless unless you pick it up and learn how to use it. Unfortunately, many Christians are weak in today's world because their sword remains unused. They are illiterate when it comes to knowing the truth of God's word. They are still babes in the Lord given to carnality rather than studying and following the precepts found in God's word. As a result, they leave themselves open to Satan's attacks. To be ready for all that God is about to do, we must pick up this powerful weapon and learn how to wield it with force and power towards its intended purposes.

Praying and being watchful in all things with all the saints is the final piece of our spiritual armor. In the early Church, most meetings were in house churches, where the saints gathered together in small clusters to pray for one another as they received teaching and instruction from each other. Gathering together in small groups gives us added protection from all the enemy's devices.

The following illustration by Jeremy Myers illustrates this. He said, "Often when seeking to advance on the field of battle, several soldiers would create a formation called a testudo, or "tortoise," in which the soldiers would gather close together in a tight, square group, with the soldiers on all four sides creating a wall of shields, and the soldiers on the inside raising their shields above to protect from arrows and rocks. In this way, the shield also helped the Roman soldiers work together as a unit. The shields protected the soldier himself and the soldier on either side of them. The soldiers, remember, worked as a band of brothers, as a unified whole,

---

[150] Hebrews 4:12

and the shields were one of the primary methods of defense for the soldiers on the shield of battle."[151]

Fully clothed in our spiritual armor, we are able and ready to go forth boldly in the battles we face, knowing that the anointing of the Holy Spirit equips us for whatever the enemy may throw our way. We are invincible. There is nothing he can do to hurt us. We have no reason to fear or cower in his presence. The Scriptures teach us that God gave us authority to trample over all the power of the enemy. We are invincible because we operate out of the stronghold of God's righteousness.

Poem: Power to Destroy Works of Darkness

With the powers of darkness at work, cultures crumble in mass.
As confusion and anger rule, ruination spreads across the globe.
As the anointed ones consider, righteous indignation rises.
With armor given, they rise to trample the enemy with fortitude.
Knowing he's powerless and unable to hurt, they are renewed.

Given entirely to God's word, the anointed arise strengthened.
With the belt of truth, they disarm flagrant lies hurled freely.
Beaten down by lies, pillars of truth are diligently restored.
Meditating and studying God's truth, they prosper mightily.
Nowhere to stand amid truth, the enemy stands defeated.

With the breastplate of righteousness, guilt-free, they attack.
Free from condemnation and doubt, they're no longer held back.
Knowing their sin became His sin, they stand guiltless before Him.
Standing in His righteousness, all weight lifted, they give praise.
Without restraint, empowered, they go, destroying works of darkness.

With feet shod with the gospel, they boldly speak, giving thanks.
Carrying the good news of the gospel everywhere, many join ranks.
As the army multiplies, revival fires spread rapidly across the globe.
Lost in confusion, the demonized swing violently, unable to afflict.
Marching in step, the anointed engage mightily in spiritual conflict.

With shields of faith, they march, destroying strongholds as directed.
Quenching fiery darts with their shields, the anointed stand protected.
Into Satan's domains, they go, destroying his works of darkness.

---

[151] https://redeeminggod.com/ephesians_6_16

The Rise of the Anointed Ones – Fortifying our Stronghold with Armor

From faith to faith, they overcome, dismantling strongholds everywhere.
As the tide turns, freedom rings worldwide, sparking revival fires.

The helmet of salvation placed; they wallow in fruits of righteousness.
With the benefits of salvation, they're mindful of His graciousness.
In forgiveness and healing, redeemed from destruction, they give praise.
Crowned with loving kindness and tender mercies, they follow His ways.
Their youth renewed like the eagle's; they realize nothing is too difficult.

They rush into battle with swords in hand to reclaim what was lost.
The Word sharp as a two-edged sword, they break through to reclaim.
Breaking into Satan's domain, they run, taking back all stolen.
With a sense of invincibility upon them, the anointed ones reclaim.
With the restoration of all completed, they await the return of their King.

Prayer

I thank you, Heavenly Father, for all that You have poured into my life, especially the weapons needed to wage an effective warfare against the enemy of our faith. Help me be faithful to put on and use each part of the armor You have given. Teach me how to use each piece effectively as I go about my day.

~

As you are diligent to put on each piece of armor, may the Lord give you the strength to fortify your stronghold and become invincible in Him.

Day 39

Staying the Course

The journey we are on is not a sprint. It's a lifetime race filled with many obstacles, traps, pitfalls, and unexpected twists and turns with the potential of throwing us off course. However, we are encouraged to be steadfast until the end. Though tempted to give up at times, we must hold fast to the path no matter how difficult it may seem at times.

Hebrews 3:14 *For we have become partakers of Christ if we hold the beginning of our confidence steadfast to the end.*

As we rely on the Holy Spirit to continually guide us, we will stay the course with our confidence intact until the end. As we are faithful to rely on His sufficiency, He will faithfully guide us through every obstacle, temptation, and trial to keep us safe and secure as we move forward in His grace. We must always keep in mind that we have a partner who is our helper at every stage of the race. Relying on the Him is a fundamental key to enduring to the end.

When considering the challenge to stay the course, we must remain as enthusiastic and full of zeal today as when we first encountered Jesus. Our first love experiences will wane at times, which is why Paul encouraged us never to lack enthusiasm or diligence but to be fervent in the spirit while serving the Lord. We must continually stir our passion and zeal by faithfully pressing forward in all that He has for us. As we are faithful to use the gifts and callings God gives for each stage of our journey, we maintain the zeal and passion for not lagging in enthusiasm no matter what circumstances we may encounter along the way. He is Jehovah-Jireh, our provider.

To continually stir our passion and zeal involves reminding ourselves, daily, what Christ accomplished in us through His suffering to impart life into our beleaguered spirits. Without Him going to the cross to pay the penalty for our sins, we would be most miserable and lost without hope in this world. Because He first loved us, we love Him. When we are faithful to remind ourselves daily of what He's accomplished in our lives, we have a heart of thanksgiving for all He's done for us. By giving thanks, daily, we continually stir our passion and zeal towards Him and what He desires to accomplish in us as we move forward. It's a crucial part of what gives us the confidence and the eagerness to stay the course He has fashioned for each of us.

Maintaining our passion and zeal will also involve understanding how His creative powers work in us. It consists of a discovery process into the uniqueness of who we are in relationship to our personality, gifts, talents, and where our passion lies. It's essential to keep in mind that God created us with a purpose in mind. What is the purpose the Father has imparted to you? You were skillfully, wonderfully designed, and fashioned by God to be a part of His plans and purposes for humankind.

> When considering the challenge to stay the course, we must remain as enthusiastic and full of zeal today as when we first encountered Jesus. Our first love experiences will wane at times, which is why Paul encouraged us never to lack enthusiasm or diligence but to be fervent in the spirit while serving the Lord.

***Psalms 139:14-17** I will praise You, for I am fearfully and wonderfully made; marvelous are Your works, and that my soul knows very well. ¹⁵ My frame was not hidden from You when I was made in secret and skillfully wrought in the lowest parts of the earth. ¹⁶ Your eyes saw my substance, being yet unformed. And in Your book, they all were written, the days fashioned for me when as yet there were none of them. ¹⁷ How precious also are Your thoughts to me, O God! How great is the sum of them!"*

As you discover all of God's creative abilities in relationship to who you are, you become a passionate person filled with a zeal that continually keeps you stirred up in things of God relating to His purposes on the earth. It keeps you staying the course in all that God wrote in His great book about what He has planned for your life.

Therefore, as we continually give Jesus thanksgiving for all that He suffered on our behalf and we set our hearts to discover the uniqueness of who He has created us to be, we won't have any problem staying the course. We will endure to the end as He urged us to do.

***Hebrews 4:14** Seeing then that we have a great High Priest who has passed through the heavens, Jesus the Son of God, let us hold fast our confession.*

Poem: Called to a Life-Long Journey

Called to a life-long journey, pressing, we stay on track.
Obstacles and traps, with twists and turns, we navigate.
With the prize before us, we endure for His sake.
The cross before us, we embrace wholeheartedly.
Tempted to give up at times, we move forward steadfastly,

The Spirit, as our trusted guide, we stay the course.
Knowing what's before us, we rely on Him extensively.
Refreshed along the way, we gain strength and vitality.
Knowing we have such a helper, we run rigorously.
Secure in His grace, in Him, we trust thoroughly.

Pushing forward with renewed zeal, we stay the course.
Reminded of past victories, passion inflames to renew.
Giving thanks to Him above, His Spirit refreshes anew.
Hearts filled with praise; we worship Him who restores.
Renewed and encouraged with joy, we run and do not tire.

Discovering His creative powers at work, we stay the course.
Knowing we are fearfully and wonderfully made, faith enforces.
From faith to faith, He leads in destiny and purpose to fulfill.
Fervent in the spirit, gifts discharge to enhance exploration.
Eyes of understanding opened; revelation produces activation.

His thoughts wonderful towards us, we stay the course.
Filled with thoughts of peace; we stay connected to the source.
His thoughts revealing the uniqueness of who we are, passion fills.
As passion ignites, His thoughts toward us magnify His greatness.
His majesty filling our hearts to the end, we shine in magnificence.

Prayer

Help me, Lord, to remain faithful to You all the years of my life. Help me continually stir Your zeal and passion towards Your purposes that I never lack in enthusiasm and zeal.

~

May God bless you richly as you work out your salvation in fear and trembling. May you enter all that He wrote about you in His great book. As we run the race with endurance, may it cause us to say, as the apostle Paul said at the end of his life, "I have fought the good fight, I have finished the race, I have kept the faith." May this be our testimony as well.

Day 40

The Second Coming of Jesus Christ

The Second Coming of the Lord Jesus Christ is the Church's great hope. As Christians, we look forward to this event with great anticipation. The Second Coming gives us a striking expectation of the great and glorious things that will take place at His appearance. It also provides us with a faith picture of how we will be changed in the twinkling of an eye to be wholly conformed into Christ's image.[152] We will be delivered and freed from the bondage of this flesh, as the passage below details.

1 Corinthians 15:54-57 So when this corruptible has put on incorruption, and this mortal has put on immortality, then shall be brought to pass the saying that is written: "Death is swallowed up in victory." 55 "O Death, where is your sting? O Hades where is your victory?" 56 The sting of death is sin, and the strength of sin is the law. 57 But thanks be to God, who gives us the victory through our Lord Jesus Christ.

There are many views amongst Christians as to when Jesus will return. The objective here is not to lift one view above another, but to simply look at the fact that Jesus will return in the near future and how we must prepare ourselves for this momentous event the Church has been anticipating since the ascension of Jesus to the Father following His resurrection from the dead. Almost every generation since Jesus ascended into heaven has expected His return. No one knows when He will return. However, Jesus and other writers of the Scriptures have given us signs that point towards the season of His coming.

---

[152] 1 Corinthians 15:52

The Rise of the Anointed Ones – The Second Coming of Christ

Acts 1:9-11** Now when He had spoken these things, while they watched, **He was taken up, and a cloud received Him out of their sight.** ¹⁰And while they looked steadfastly toward heaven as He went up, behold, two men stood by them in white apparel, ¹¹who also said, "Men of Galilee, why do you stand gazing up into heaven? **This same Jesus, who was taken up from you into heaven, will so come in like manner as you saw Him go into heaven."

Let's keep in mind that no one knows the day nor the hour, but that doesn't mean we should be ignorant of the season as Jesus reminded us, when He said, *"But of that day and **hour,** no one knows, not even the angels of heaven, but My Father only.*[153]

Even though we won't know the day or the hour of His return, God expects us to be aware of our seasons. We see where Jesus rebuked the Pharisees and the Sadducees for not being able to discern the signs of the times.

Matthew 16:2-3** He answered and said to them, "When it is evening you say, 'It will be fair weather, for the sky is red'; ³ "and in the morning, 'It will be foul weather today, for the sky is red and threatening.' Hypocrites! **You know how to discern the face of the sky, but you cannot discern the signs of the times.

Jesus wants us to be like the sons of Issachar, who understood their times, and knew what Israel should do.[154] There must be those in the Church today who understand the times, who also know what the Church should do to prepare for the second coming of Christ. Many of the signs Jesus and other Bible writers said would precede His coming seem to be apparent in our current season of time. It could be that we are now in the season Jesus spoke of concerning the coming birth pangs

***Mark 13:7-8** "But when you hear of wars and rumors of wars, do not be troubled; for such things must happen, but the end is not yet. ⁸ "For nation will rise against nation and kingdom against kingdom. And there will be earthquakes in various places, and there will be famines and troubles. These are the beginnings of sorrows.*

***2 Timothy 3:1-5** But know this, that in the last days perilous times will come: ² For men will be lovers of themselves, lovers of money, boasters, proud, blasphemers, disobedient to parents, unthankful, unholy, ³ unloving, unforgiving, slanderers, without self-control, brutal, despisers of good, ⁴ traitors, headstrong, haughty, lovers of pleasure rather than lovers of God, ⁵ having a form of godliness but denying its power. And from such people turn away!*

---

[153] Matthew 24:36
[154] 1 Chronicles 12:32

The Rise of the Anointed Ones – The Second Coming of Christ

With an understanding that we are most likely at the beginning of the birth pangs Jesus spoke of, we must make sure we prepare ourselves for His coming, lest we get caught sleeping. We don't want to be caught unprepared like the foolish virgins Jesus spoke of in His parable.[155]

Luke 21:34-36 *"But take heed to yourselves, lest your hearts be weighed down with carousing, drunkenness, and cares of this life, and that Day come on you unexpectedly. ³⁵"For it will come as a snare on all those who dwell on the face of the whole earth. ³⁶"Watch therefore,* ***and pray always that you may be counted worthy to escape all these things*** *that will come to pass, and to stand before the Son of Man."*

Before the Second Coming of Christ, the great challenge for the Christian will be to maintain a state of readiness. Because, when Jesus returns, He's coming for a bride that has made herself ready and is full of faith.

Revelation 19:7 *"Let us be glad and rejoice and give Him glory, for the marriage of the Lamb has come, and His wife has made herself* ***ready****."*

Matthew 25:10 *"And while they went to buy, the bridegroom came, and those who were* ***ready*** *went in with him to the wedding; and the door was shut.*

Jesus' parable of the ten virgins reveals that the determining factor in being ready is the amount of oil in our vessels. Oil is always symbolic of the Holy Spirit in the Bible. Therefore, we must have an ongoing vibrant relationship with the Holy Spirit, keeping ourselves stirred up in the faith if we want to be among those who will be ready when the Bridegroom comes for His bride.

The following gives you a good reminder on how to keep yourself stirred up in the faith and in a state of readiness:

- Baptism of the Holy Spirit – *Maintains your oil supply.*[156]
- Build a Strong Word Foundation – *Lamps represent God's Word.*[157]
- Walk in the fear of the Lord. – *This is what gives wisdom.*[158]
- Put on the garments of the new nature – *This destroys the old nature.*[159]
- Purpose to walk in love – *Love is what holds everything together.*[160]

---

[155] Matthew 25:1-10
[156] 1 John 2:20,27 – from Strong's Concordance <G5548> (chrio); an *unguent* or *smearing*, i.e. (figurative) the special *endowment* ("chrism") of the Holy Spirit :- anointing, unction.
[157] Psalm 119:105, Hebrews 6:1-3 – foundations truths needed to go on to maturity.
[158] 2 Corinthians 7:1 – perfect holiness in the fear of God
[159] Ephesians 4:20-24 – the new nature vs. the old nature.
[160] Colossians 3:14 – Love the bond of perfection.

The Rise of the Anointed Ones – The Second Coming of Christ

- Learn to Accept Trials and Tribulations with Joy – *This is what matures us.*[161]

We are in a season of laboring together with the Lord. However, a day is coming when we cease from our part in the process. God will then perfect in us what He began. He is the author and finisher of our salvation.[162] Until then, we must remain steadfast, immovable, always abounding in the work of the Lord, knowing that our labor is not in vain in the Lord.[163]

Poem: The Second Coming of Christ

On His white horse, He prepares to ride with sword in hand.
Prepared for vengeance, He comes to those who disdain.
As the last trumpet blows, reins in hand, He mounts up.
Gathering the righteous together, they're caught up.
No longer chained to earthly realities, they're now freed.

From the four winds, He gathers them for the great battle.
With new celestial bodies, His saints are forever changed.
In the twinkling of an eye, they meet Him in the air.
As corruptible puts on incorruption, they're made anew.
Leaving behind the sting of death, they embrace victory.

Ready to engage in the great battle, they mount up, prepared.
As the seventh angel pours his bowl, a loud shout is heard.
A great noise heard, thunderings and lightning alert.
A shout from the temple signals. "It is done!" The time is now.
As a great and mighty earthquake shakes the land, He's ready.

As every island and mountain disappear, they ride together.
With Armageddon their destination, senses fill with expectation.
Riding to the great battle, He who rides the white horse leads.
In flaming fire, they come, punishing with everlasting destruction.
Into the bottomless pit, the serpent of old is bound and thrown.

A thousand years, he's bound until loosed again for a short season.
With the kingdoms of this world now His, He sets up His throne.
Dining together, they sit with the patriarchs and prophets of old.
For a thousand years, they dwell in peace in His presence.
Building, planting, and ruling, they wait the new heavens and earth.

---

[161] James 1:2 – Count it all joy
[162] Philippians 1:6, Ephesians 5, Romans 9:28,
[163] 1 Corinthians 15:58

The Rise of the Anointed Ones – The Second Coming of Christ

With walls of Jasper, New Jerusalem comes as a city of pure gold.
Beyond comprehension, they see, hear, and sense all that's prepared.
Basking in His presence, their hearts continually bring forth praise.
Worshipping Him who was worthy to loose the seals, they rejoice.
Forever, to the King of Kings who was slain, they honor and praise.

Prayer

Heavenly Father, help me not to be caught sleeping when You appear. Continually pour your anointing oil into my life to keep me steadfast in the work of Your kingdom. Thank you for the hope of Your second coming and the inspiration it deposits into my life.

About the Author

Ken Birks is an ordained Pastor/Teacher in the Body of Christ. He functioned as an elder, a staff pastor, and Bible teacher at The Rock of Roseville in California for the past 20 years. He is presently semi-retired with a writing ministry and serves as a wedding officiant in the Sacramento region. Before this, Ken was the Senior Pastor of Golden Valley Christian Center, a Spirit-filled, non-denominational church in Roseville, for twelve years.k

Ken attended and graduated from the Charismatic Bible College of Anchorage. He came into the relationship with Apostle Dick Benjamin, then the Pastor of Abbott Loop Christian Center (ALCC) in Anchorage, Alaska.

Aside from The Lord Jesus Christ, the core of Ken's spiritual being and the person he's become is a direct result from the influence and teaching he received from Dick Benjamin for more than 40 years." Other influences have been Bob Mumford from Life Changers and, in the past 20+ years, Pastor Francis Anfuso of The Rock of Roseville.

Ken has been married to Lydia for 43 years. They have two adult children and consider them their highest calling, along with the many teens and children they have been foster or surrogate parents to over the past 30+ years.

Check out Ken's internet ministry called "Sowing Seeds of Faith" located at kenbirks.com. Sowing Seeds of Faith reaches over 5500 unique visitors a month with free Bible studies, devotional poetry, sermon outlines, audio, and video messages, podcasts, and other Bible study materials to help equip saints for the work of the ministry.

Books by Ken Birks

Treasures From Above

These devotionals are designed to enhance your relationship with the Lord Jesus Christ in all aspects of your walk. The intent is to draw you into a deeper understanding of how the Holy Spirit and God's Word work together to conform you into the image of Christ. The aspect that separates this book from other devotionals is that each devotional ends with a biblically inspired poem that encapsulates the essence of the devotional.

Prophetic Purposes and the Zeal of the Lord

Do you believe worldwide revival is possible? Imagine what it will be like when the Church rises in the glory spoken of by Isaiah, the prophet. Just as God in His sovereignty brought forth the Messiah according to the timing of Daniel's prophecy, He will bring forth the prophetic purpose of a worldwide revival according to His timing. God's people, whom He planted in every city, village, town, and countryside throughout the world, will stand up as the vast army just as Ezekiel prophesied. His prophetic purpose will be fulfilled.

Treasures of the Heart
Prose and Poetry Refreshing the Soul

As you read through the devotional prose and poetry found in this book, you will find a beautiful blend of timeless truths fitly applied to today's culture and challenges that fill your heart with treasures from above. The Heavenly insights will challenge you to grow in the knowledge of the Son of God.

The majestic flow from one poem to the next contains powerful prophetic wisdom and revelation that will fill your hearts and minds with the wonderful treasures God intends you to enjoy.

Books by Ken Birks

The Adventures of Space and Hobo

The Adventures of Space and Hobo tells the story of Ken's nomadic life after Vietnam. The book explores the on-the-ground confusion and chaos of the Vietnam War and its effects on a generation and those who served. Named "Space" by a new friend, Hobo, The story takes us step by step along the path of awakening a lost soul on his way to finding an understanding of himself, his path, and the meaning of his life. The story takes us step by step along the path of awakening a lost soul on his way to understanding himself, his path, and the meaning of his life.

The Journey: Discovering the Invisible Path

The Journey gives you a glimpse into the path God has purposed for your life. Whether you are starting your journey, in the middle, or you've detoured and lost your way, this book will help you. This practical guidebook will shine the light on the invisible path that leads to God's goodness and experiencing His kingdom within. It will lead you to discover the most incredible adventure of your life.

Quote from Pastor Francis Anfuso, KLOVE Personality– "Ken makes complex concepts simple and masterfully unpacks the Bible's greatest mysteries. He provides a sure foundation upon which to build a lifetime of insight."

See another review of this book on page 181.

For more information on these books and other materials by Ken Birks, please visit www.booksbyken

Workbooks by Ken Birks

Biblical Perspectives Course

This course features lessons designed to give you a solid Biblical foundation in the elementary truths of God's Word. It has three things in mind: building doctrinal foundations, developing godly character, and helping you discover and find the destiny and purpose God has for your life. Please see the following website for more information and Lesson Titles:

www.kenbirks.com/perspectives-both/

More Biblical Perspectives Course

This course features lessons focused on three major areas of our Christian growth - doctrine, character, and destiny.

These lessons are designed to give you the Biblical understanding to strengthen your Christian foundation and take you on a deeper walk with God.

Please see the following website for more information and lesson titles:

www.kenbirks.com/perspectives-both/

Small-Group Lesson Guides

Twenty-five Lessons to help you discover Jesus in your midst during small group Bible studies.

Please see the following website for complete information and titles:

www.kenbirks.com/discipleship/lesson-guides.htm

Reviews and References

David Fredrickson, Sr. Pastor (Retired), Evangel Christian Fellowship, Sacramento, CA

Most true followers of Christ would agree that we are witnessing a time when self-serving Christianity is reaping the whirlwind of disunity, confusion, and fruitlessness. It is past time to listen to the voice of reason merely. Instead, we must respond with renewed minds, hearts, and actions.

Rise of the Anointed Ones is like a voice in the wilderness calling God's beloved away from all that distracts to Him who is jealous for His bride. The reader who hears and responds will bring joy to the heart of God and encouragement to others who have put their hand to the plow.

Edward Becker, Senior Pastor, Naches Valley Community Church, Yakima, WA; Vice President, Antioch World Missions

"RISE OF THE ANOINTED ONES" by Ken Birks is more than a daily devotional in the hands of the reader. This work is filled with Biblical truths and spiritual revelation that flow from a heart passionate for the Savior and His precious Bride, the Church.

Today, there are hundreds of devotionals available – from Oswald Chambers to A.W. Tozier, Anne Graham Lotz, and many more.

Ken Birks has written a masterpiece of superb continuity. Each daily devotional I read, along with the poem, and special prayer, became my favorite in the whole book – until I read the next one.

As I finished the manuscript, I realized each devotional revealed timely end-time strategies to enlighten, equip, and inspire the believer. Each devotional also challenges the reader to grow, mature, and pursue the highest level of Christian conduct.

The majestic flow from theme to theme contains powerful prophetic revelation, as God calls His end-time warriors to arise. I was also amazed by the poems that followed each devotional – the words were Davidic and musical – they flowed like a delightful stream with heavenly impartations.

Reviews and References

I will give "RISE OF THE ANOINTED ONES" a privileged place at our church book table. I will highly recommend it to everyone in our fellowship – as well as to the unbeliever.

I have known Ken Birks for forty years and have enjoyed a wonderful friendship while sharing in the work of the Lord. I believe this book will bless and encourage multitudes. – *Pastor Edward Becker*

Dr. Jay Zinn, Founder of The Discipleship Group, a national and international program for developing and equipping disciples to become disciple-makers.

"There are few authors who can take theology and turn it into a devotional series of divine, inspiring nuggets and poetry. Ken Birks is an author who penetrates your heart and soul to know God better."
— *Dr. Jay Zinn*

Dr. Jim Feeney, Former Sr. Pastor. Webmaster at Pentecostal Bible Studies and Free Pentecostal Sermons Central

"I've known Pastor Ken Birks for several decades. He and I have worked in various ministerial capacities in the same family of churches. Ken is held in extremely high esteem among our many pastoral colleagues. He is a minister with a strong grasp of the Word of God, a wide variety of administrative skills, a heart for souls, a proven experiential familiarity with the gifts of the Holy Spirit, and an unwavering commitment to the work of the Lord."

John Dubler, Senior Pastor of Good Shepherd Bible Chapel, Fort Collins, CO

"Ken Birks is an extremely effective teacher of the Scriptures. He combines a healthy respect for the Word with enthusiasm and personal experiences that match his teaching. Ken is a man of unimpeachable integrity, and his longevity in the Body of Christ as a pastor gives credence to the message of hope and encouragement that he brings to all."

Reviews and References

Doug Hartline, Information/Technology Director, University of California

When thinking about reading a devotional, one must ask themselves two questions – is it relevant, and what makes it stand apart from the myriad of devotionals one can choose from? From my perspective, devotionals can be vital tools in improving upon our quiet time experience with God. They should be able to bring scriptural insight to us. Scripture is far more important than the words of even the most famous of authors, for it is Scripture that penetrates our souls with God's wisdom and daily guidance. Ken's work herein ensures that God's Word takes center stage and holds the most important place within it so that it remains both timeless and relevant.

It is the incredible prose and poetry, however, that separates his devotional books and makes them stand apart from the others. Poetry can shine a light on God's Word from a different angle, in a way that helps us to look at it in a much deeper and often more profound way. It provides us with a unique ability to understand and appreciate God's Word in ways we may never have thought of before. We are suddenly confronted with beauty and clarity to our perceptions of our world and God's Kingdom.

I have just read a book entitled *"The Journey"* written by Kenneth L. Birks. I have known my friend, Ken Birks, for 38 years. He is a man of absolute integrity. He is a diligent student of the Bible. He is a Holy Spirit-filled teacher. This book contains many scriptures referred to and identified at the bottom of the pages. In short, this book is based on the Bible. I believe Ken is also an example of his writing in this book. I recommend this book to individuals, small group leaders, pastors, churches, Bible schools, and seminaries. *"The Journey"* will help make disciples out of believers. —*Richard C. Benjamin Sr., Apostle/Pastor/retired*

Online Connections

www.kenbirks.com
Sowing Seeds of Faith, Bible Studies and More

www.kenbirks.com/videos
Sermon Videos by Ken Birks

www.straitarrow.net
Bible Studies, Podcasts, Seminars, and More

www.straitarrow.net/devotional-poetry
Biblical Devotional Poetry

www.straitarrow.net/Newsletters
Bi-Monthly Newsletters

www.booksbyken.com
How to order Ken's books and materials

www.sacramento-wedding-officiants.com
Wedding Officiating

Email: klbirks@gmail.com

X Formerly Twitter: @klbirks

Instagram: kenlbirks

www.ingramcontent.com/pod-product-compliance
Lightning Source LLC
Chambersburg PA
CBHW050318120526
44592CB00014B/1956